Beethoven's Letters 1790 - 1826

Volume 2

From the Collection of Dr. Ludwig Nohl

By Ludwig van Beethoven

Translated by Lady Grace Jane Wallace

Published by Pantianos Classics

ISBN-13: 978-1-78987-414-3

First published in 1866

Contents

Third Part - Life's Troubles and Close - 1823 to 1827 61

Second Part - Life's Mission - 1815-1822.

(Continued.)

216 - To Steiner & Co.

The Adjutant's innocence is admitted, and there is an end of it!

We beg you to be so good as to send us two copies in score of the Symphony in A. We likewise wish to know when we may expect a copy of the Sonata for Baroness von Ertmann, as she leaves this, most probably, the day after tomorrow.

No. 3--I mean the enclosed note--is from a musical friend in Silesia, not a rich man, for whom I have frequently had my scores written out. He wishes to have these works of Mozart in his library; as my servant, however, has the good fortune, by the grace of God, to be one of the greatest blockheads in the world (which is saying a good deal), I cannot make use of him for this purpose. Be so kind therefore as to send to Herr ---- (for the Generalissimus can have no dealings with a petty tradesman), and desire him to write down the price of each work and send it to me with my two scores in A, and also an answer to my injunction about Ertmann, as early to-day as you can (presto, prestissimo!)--nota bene, the finale to be a march in double-quick time. I recommend the best execution of these orders, so that no further obstacle may intervene to my recovery.

L. VAN BEETHOVEN,

The best generalissimus for the good,
But the devil himself for the bad!

217 - To Steiner.

The Lieutenant-General is requested to send his Diabolum, that I may tell him myself my opinion of the "Battle," which is printed in the vilest manner. There is much to be altered.

THE G----S.

218 - To Tobias Haslinger.

MY GOOD ADJUTANT,--

Best of all little fellows! Do see again about that house, and get it for me. I am very anxious also to procure the treatise on education. It is of some importance to me to be able to compare my own opinions on this subject with those of others, and thus still further improve them. As for our juvenile Adjutant, I think I shall soon have hit on the right system for his education. Your

CONTRA FA,
Manu propria.

219 - To the High-Born Herr Haslinger, Honorary Member of the Höfen Grabens and Pater Noster Gässchen.

BEST OF ALL PRINTERS AND ENGRAVERS,--

Be kinder than kind, and throw off a hundred impressions of the accompanying small plate.[1] I will repay you threefold and fourfold. Farewell!
Your
BEETHOVEN.

*[**Note 1:** This is possibly the humorous visiting-card that Beethoven sometimes sent to his friends, with the inscription Wir bleiben die Alten ("We are the same as ever"), and on reversing the card, a couple of asses stared them in the face! Frau Eyloff told me of a similar card that her brother Schindler once got from Beethoven on a New Year's day.]*

220 - To Baroness Dorothea von Ertmann.[1]

Feb. 23, 1817.

MY DEAR AND VALUED DOROTHEA CECILIA,--

You have no doubt often misjudged me, from my apparently forbidding manner; much of this arose from circumstances, especially in earlier days, when my nature was less understood than at present. You know the manifestations of those self-elected apostles who promote their interests by means very different from those of the true Gospel. I did not wish to be included in that number. Receive now what has been long intended for you,[2] and may it serve as a proof of my admiration of your artistic talent, and likewise of yourself! My not having heard you recently at Cz---- [Czerny's] was owing to indisposition, which at last appears to be giving way to returning health.

I hope soon to hear how you get on at St. Polten [where her husband's regiment was at that time quartered], and whether you still think of your admirer and friend,
L. VAN BEETHOVEN.

My kindest regards to your excellent husband.

*[**Note 1:** It was admitted that she played Beethoven's compositions with the most admirable taste and feeling. Mendelssohn thought so in 1830 at Milan, and mentions it in his Letters from Italy and Switzerland.]*

*[**Note 2:** Undoubtedly the Sonata dedicated to her, Op. 101.]*

221 - To Zmeskall.

DEAR Z.,--

I introduce to your notice the bearer of this, young Bocklet, who is a very clever violin-player. If you can be of any service to him through your acquaintances, do your best for him, especially as he is warmly recommended to me from Prague.[1]

As ever, your true friend,
BEETHOVEN.

*[**Note 1:** Carl Maria Bocklet, a well-known and distinguished pianist in Vienna. He told me himself that he came for the first time to Vienna in 1817, where he stayed six weeks. On April 8th he gave a violin concert in the Kleine Redoutensaale. He brought a letter of introduction to Beethoven, from his friend Dr. Berger in Prague.]*

222 - To Steiner & Co.

The Lieutenant-General is desired to afford all aid and help to the young artist Bocklet from Prague. He is the bearer of this note, and a virtuoso on the violin. We hope that our command will be obeyed, especially as we subscribe ourselves, with the most vehement regard, your
GENERALISSIMUS.

223 - To G. Del Rio.

I only yesterday read your letter attentively at home. I am prepared to give up Carl to you at any moment, although I think it best not to do so till after the examination on Monday; but I will send him sooner if you wish it. At all events it would be advisable afterwards to remove him from here, and to send him to Mölk, or some place where he will neither see nor hear anything more of his abominable mother. When he is in the midst of strangers, he will meet with less support, and find that he can only gain the love and esteem of others by his own merits.

In haste, your
BEETHOVEN.

224 - To G. Del Rio.

I request you, my dear friend, to inquire whether in any of the houses in your vicinity there are lodgings to be had at Michaelmas, consisting of a few rooms. You must not fail to do this for me to-day or to-morrow.

Your friend,
L. VAN BEETHOVEN.

P.S.--N.B. Though I would gladly profit by your kind offer of living in your garden-house, various circumstances render this impossible. My kind regards to all your family.

225 - To G. Del Rio.

HOUSE OF GIANNATASIO!--

The treatise on the piano is a general one,--that is, it is a kind of compendium. Besides, I am pleased with the Swiss [probably Weber, a young musician who had been recommended to him], but the "Guaden" is no longer the fashion.

In haste, the devoted servant and friend of the Giannatasio family,

BEETHOVEN.

226 - To G. Del Rio.

You herewith receive through Carl, my dear friend, the ensuing quarter due to you. I beg you will attend more to the cultivation of his feelings and kindness of heart, as the latter in particular is the lever of all that is good; and no matter how a man's kindly feeling may be ridiculed or depreciated, still our greatest authors, such as Goethe and others, consider it an admirable quality; indeed, many maintain that without it no man can ever be very distinguished, nor can any depth of character exist.

My time is too limited to say more, but we can discuss verbally how in my opinion Carl ought to be treated on this point.

Your friend and servant,
L. VAN BEETHOVEN.

Alser Vorstadt--Beim Apfel, 2ter Étage,
No. 12, Leiberz, Dressmaker.

227 - To G. Del Rio.

This is at any rate the first time that it has been necessary to remind me of an agreeable duty; very pressing business connected with my art, as well as other causes, made me totally forget the account, but this shall not occur again. As for my servant bringing home Carl in the evening, the arrangement is already made. In the mean time I thank you for having been so obliging as to send your servant for him yesterday, as I knew nothing about it, so that Carl probably must otherwise have remained at Czerny's. Carl's boots are too small, and he has repeatedly complained of this; indeed, they are so bad that he can scarcely walk, and it will take some time before they can be altered to fit him. This kind of thing ruins the feet, so I beg you will not allow him to wear them again till they are made larger.

With regard to his pianoforte studies, I beg you will keep him strictly to them; otherwise his music-master would be of no use. Yesterday Carl could not play the whole day, I have repeatedly wished to hear him play over his lessons, but have been obliged to come away without doing so.

"La musica merita d'esser studiata."

Besides, the couple of hours now appointed for his music lessons are quite insufficient. I must therefore the more earnestly urge on you their being strictly adhered to. It is by no means unusual that this point should be attended to in an institute; an intimate friend of mine has also a boy at school, who is to become a professor of music, where every facility for study is afforded him; indeed, I was rather struck by finding the boy quite alone in a distant room practising, neither disturbing others, nor being himself disturbed.

I beg you will allow me to send for Carl to-morrow about half-past ten o'clock, as I wish to see what progress he has made, and to take him with me to some musicians.

I am, with all possible esteem, your friend,

L. VAN BEETHOVEN.

228 - To Czerny.

DEAR CZERNY,--

I beg you will treat Carl with as much patience as possible; for though he does not as yet get on quite as you and I could wish, still I fear he will soon do even less, because (though I do not want him to know it) he is over-fatigued by the injudicious distribution of his lesson hours. Unluckily it is not easy to alter this; so pray, however strict you may be, show him every indulgence, which will, I am sure, have also a better effect on Carl under such unfavorable circumstances.

With respect to his playing with you, when he has finally acquired the proper mode of fingering, and plays in right time, and gives the notes with tolerable correctness, you must only then first direct his attention to the mode of execution; and when he is sufficiently advanced, do not stop his playing on account of little mistakes, but only point them out at the end of the piece. Although I have myself given very little instruction, I have always followed this system, which quickly forms a musician; and this is, after all, one of the first objects of art, and less fatiguing both to master and scholar. In certain passages, like the following,--

I wish all the fingers to be used; and also in similar ones, such as these,--

so that they may go very smoothly; such passages can indeed be made to sound very perlés, or like a pearl, played by fewer fingers, but sometimes we wish for a different kind of jewel.[1] More as to this some other time. I hope that you will receive these suggestions in the same kindly spirit in which they are offered and intended. In any event I am, and ever must remain, your debtor. May my candor serve as a pledge of my wish to discharge this debt at some future day!

Your true friend,
BEETHOVEN.

*[**Note 1:** Carl Czerny relates in the Vienna A.M. Zeitung of 1845, No. 113, as follows:--"Beethoven came to me usually every day himself with the boy, and used to say to me, 'You must not think that you please me by making Carl play my works; I am not so childish as to wish anything of the kind. Give him whatever you think best.' I named Clementi. 'Yes, yes,' said he, 'Clementi is very good indeed;' and, added he, laughing, 'Give Carl occasionally what is according to rule, that he may hereafter come to what is contrary to rule.' After a hit of this sort, which he introduced into almost every speech, he used to burst into a loud peal of laughter. Having in the earlier part of his career been often reproached by the critics with his irregularities, he was in the habit of alluding to this with gay humor."]*

229 - To Czerny.

DEAR CZERNY,--

I beg you will say nothing on that particular subject at Giannatasio's, who dined with us on the day you were so good as to call on me; he requested this himself. I will tell you the reason when we meet. I hope to be able to prove my gratitude for your patience with my nephew, that I may not always remain your debtor. In haste,

Your friend,
BEETHOVEN.

230 - To Czerny.

DEAR CZERNY,--

Can you in any way assist the man I now send to you (a pianoforte maker and tuner from Baden) in selling his instruments? Though small in size, their manufacture is solid. In haste,
Your friend,
BEETHOVEN.

231 - To Zmeskall.

Wednesday, July 3, 1817.

DEAR ZMESKALL,--

I have changed my mind. It might hurt the feelings of Carl's mother to see her child in the house of a stranger, which would be more harsh than I like; so I shall allow her to come to my house to-morrow; a certain tutor at Puthon, of the name of Bihler, will also be present. I should be extremely glad if you could be with me about six o'clock, but not later. Indeed, I earnestly beg you to come, as I am desirous to show the Court that you are present, for there is no doubt that a Court Secretary will be held in higher estimation by them than a man without an official character, whatever his moral character may be!

Now, jesting apart, independent of my real affection for you, your coming will be of great service to me. I shall therefore expect you without fail. I beg you will not take my badinage amiss. I am, with sincere esteem,
Your friend,
BEETHOVEN

232 - To G. Del Rio.

Your friend has no doubt told you of my intention to send for Carl early to-morrow. I wish to place his mother in a more creditable position with the neighborhood; so I have agreed to pay her the compliment of taking her son to see her in the company of a third person. This is to be done once a month.

As to all that is past, I beg you will never allude to it again, either in speaking or writing, but forget it all--as I do.

233 - To Frau Von Streicher.

I have been occupied in arranging my papers; an immense amount of patience is required for such an affair as putting them in order, but having once summoned it to our aid we must persevere, or the matter would never be completed. My papers, both musical and unmusical, are nearly arranged at last; it was like one of the seven labors of Hercules![1]

*[**Note 1:** Ries (in Wegeler's Notizen) relates: "Beethoven placed very little value on the MSS. of his pieces written out by himself; when once engraved they were usually scattered about the anteroom, or on the floor in the middle of his apartment, together with other music. I often arranged his music for him, but the moment Beethoven began to search for any piece, it was all strewed about again."]*

234 - To Frau von Streicher.

You see what servants are! [He had gone out and taken the key with him.] Such is housekeeping! So long as I am ill, I would fain be on a different footing with those around me; for dearly as I usually love solitude, it is painful to me now, finding it scarcely possible, while taking baths and medicine, to employ myself as usual,--to which is added the grievous prospect that I may perhaps never get better. I place no confidence in my present physician, who at length pronounces my malady to be disease of the lungs. I will consider about engaging a housekeeper. If I could only have the faintest hope, in this corrupt Austrian State, of finding an honest person, the arrangement would be easily made; but--but!! [He wishes to hire a piano and pay for it in advance; the tone to be as loud as possible, to suit his defective hearing.]

Perhaps you do not know, though I have not always had one of your pianos, that since 1809 I have invariably preferred yours.

It is peculiarly hard on me to be a burden on any one, being accustomed rather to serve others than to be served by them.

235 - To Frau von Streicher.

I can only say that I am better; I thought much of death during the past night, but such thoughts are familiar to me by day also.

236 - To F. Ries,--London.

Vienna, July 9, 1817.

MY DEAR FRIEND,--

The proposals in your esteemed letter of the 9th of June are very flattering, and my reply will show you how much I value them. Were it not for my unhappy infirmities, which entail both attendance and expense, particularly on a journey to a foreign country, I would unconditionally accept the offer of the Philharmonic Society. But place yourself in my position, and consider how many more obstacles I have to contend with than any other artist, and then judge whether my demands (which I now annex) are unreasonable. I beg you will convey my conditions to the Directors of the above Society, namely:--

1. I shall be in London early in January.

2. The two grand new symphonies shall be ready by that time; to become the exclusive property of the Society.

3. The Society to give me in return 300 guineas, and 100 for my travelling expenses, which will, however, amount to much more, as I am obliged to bring a companion.

4. As I am now beginning to work at these grand symphonies for the Society, I shall expect that (on receiving my consent) they will remit me here the sum of 150 guineas, so that I may provide a carriage, and make my other preparations at once for the journey.

5. The conditions as to my non-appearance in any other public orchestra, my not directing, and the preference always to be given to the Society on the offer of equal terms by them, are accepted by me; indeed, they would at all events have been dictated by my own sense of honor.

6. I shall expect the aid of the Society in arranging one, or more, benefit concerts in my behalf, as the case may be. The very friendly feeling of some of the Directors in your valuable body, and the kind reception of my works by all the artists, is a sufficient guaranty on this point, and will be a still further inducement to me to endeavor not to disappoint their expectations.

7. I request that I may receive the assent to and confirmation of these terms, signed by three Directors in the name of the Society. You may easily imagine how much I rejoice at the thoughts of becoming acquainted with the worthy Sir George Smart [Music Director], and seeing you and Mr. Neate again; would that I could fly to you myself instead of this letter!

Your sincere well wisher and friend,

LUDWIG VAN BEETHOVEN.

[P.S. ON A SEPARATE SHEET OF PAPER.]

DEAR RIES,--

I cordially embrace you! I have purposely employed another hand in my answer to the Society, that you might read it more easily, and present it to them. I place the most implicit reliance on your kindly feelings toward me. I hope that the Philharmonic Society may accept my proposals, and they may rest assured that I shall employ all my energies to fulfil in the most satisfactory manner the flattering commission of so eminent a society of artists. What is the strength of your orchestra? How many violins, &c.? Have you one or two sets of wind instruments? Is the concert room large and sonorous?

237 - To Zmeskall.

NUSSDORF, July 23, 1817.

MY DEAR GOOD ZMESKALL,--

I shall soon see you again in town. What is the proper price for fronting a pair of boots? I have to pay my servant for this, who is always running about.

I am really in despair at being condemned by my defective hearing to pass the greater part of my life with this most odious class of people, and to be in some degree dependent on them. To-morrow, early, my servant will call on you, and bring me back a sealed answer.

238 - To Zmeskall.

August 12, 1817.

MY DEAR GOOD Z.,--

I heard of your indisposition with great regret. As for myself, I am often in despair, and almost tempted to put an end to my life, for all these remedies seem to have no end. May God have compassion on me, for I look upon my-self to be as good as lost! I have a great deal to say to you. That this servant is a thief, I cannot doubt--he must be sent away; my health requires living at home and greater comfort. I shall be glad to have your opinion on this point. If my condition is not altered, instead of being in London I shall probably be in my grave. I thank God that the thread of my life will soon be spun out.

In haste, your
BEETHOVEN.

N.B. I wish you to buy me a quarter of a yard of green wax-cloth, green on both sides. It seems incredible that I have not been able to get anything of the kind from these green people here. It is far.... [illegible].

[X. brought the Trio in C minor (Op. 1, No. 3) to show to Beethoven, having arranged it as a quintet for stringed instruments (published by Artaria as Op. 104). Beethoven evidently discovered a good many faults in the work; still, the undertaking had sufficient attractions to induce him to correct it himself, and to make many changes in it. A very different score was thus of course produced from that of X., on the cover of whose work the genial master, in a fit of good humor, inscribed with his own hand the following title:--

A Terzet arranged as a Quintet,
by Mr. Well-meaning,
translated from the semblance into the reality of five parts, and exalted from the depths of wretchedness to a certain degree of excellence, by Mr. Goodwill.

Vienna, Aug. 14, 1817.

N.B. The original three-part score of the Quintet has been sacrificed as a solemn burnt-offering to the subterranean gods.] [1]

*[**Note 1:** This Quintet appeared as Op. 104 at Artaria's in Vienna.]*

239 - To Frau von Streicher.

When we next meet, you will be surprised to hear what I have in the mean time learned. My poor Carl was only misled for the moment; but there are men who are brutes, and of this number is the priest here, who deserves to be well cudgelled.

240 - To G. Del Rio.

August 19, 1817.

I unluckily received your letter yesterday too late, for she had already been here; otherwise I would have shown her to the door, as she richly deserved. I sincerely thank Fraulein N. for the trouble she took in writing down the gossip of this woman. Though an enemy to all tattling and gossip, still this is of importance to us; so I shall write to her, and also give her letter to me to Herr A.S. [Advocate Schönauer?] I may possibly have let fall some words in her presence in reference to the recent occurrence, and the irregularity on your part, but I cannot in the slightest degree recall ever having written to her about you.

It was only an attempt on her side to exasperate you against me; and thus to influence you and obtain more from you, in the same way that she formerly reported to me all sorts of things that you had said about me; but I took no heed of her talk. On this recent occasion I wished to try whether she might not be improved by a more patient and conciliatory mode of conduct: I imparted my intention to Herr A.S., but it has utterly failed; and on Sunday I made up my mind to adhere to the former necessary severity, as even during the glimpse she had of Carl, she contrived to inoculate him with some of her venom. In short, we must be guided by the zodiac, and only allow her to see Carl twelve times a year, and then barricade her so effectually that she cannot smuggle in even a pin, whether he is with you or me, or with a third person. I really thought that by entirely complying with her wishes, it might have been an incitement to her to improve, and to acknowledge my complete unselfishness.

Perhaps I may see you to-morrow. Frau S. can order the shoes and stockings and all that Carl requires, and I will remit her the money at once. I beg that you will always order and buy anything Carl ought to have, without any reference to me, merely informing me of the amount, which I will forthwith discharge, without waiting for the end of the quarter. I will take care that Carl has a new coat for the next examination.

One thing more. The mother affects to receive her information from a person in your house. If you cannot arrange with Czerny to bring Carl home, he must not go at all; "trau, schau, wem!" [trust not till you try.] The only impression that his mother ought to make on Carl is what I have already told him,--namely, to respect her as his mother, but not to follow her example in any respect; he must be strongly warned against this.

Yours truly,

L. V. BEETHOVEN.

241 - To Zmeskall.

Sept. 11, 1817.

DEAR Z.,--

The answer from London arrived yesterday [see No. 236], but in English. Do you know any one who could translate it verbally for us? In haste,

Your

BEETHOVEN.

242 - To Zmeskall.

Oct. 20, 1817.

DEAR Z.,--

The devil himself cannot persuade your Famulus to take away the wine. Pray forgive my behavior yesterday; I intended to have asked your pardon this very afternoon. In my present condition I require indulgence from every one, for I am a poor unfortunate creature!

In haste, as ever, yours.

243 - To Zmeskall.

DEAR Z.,--

I give up the journey; at least I will not pledge myself on this point. The matter must be more maturely considered. In the mean time the work is already sent off to the Prince Regent. If they want me they can have me, and I am still at liberty to say yes! or no! Liberty!!!! what more can any one desire!!!

244 - To Zmeskall.

DEAR Z.,--

Don't be angry about my note. Are you not aware of my present condition, which is like that of Hercules with Queen Omphale??? I asked you to buy me a looking-glass like yours, which I now return, but if you do not require it, I wish you would send yours back to me to-day, for mine is broken. Farewell, and do not write in such high-flown terms about me, for never have I felt so strongly as now the strength and the weakness of human nature.

Continue your regard for me.

245 - To Frau von Streicher.

The Autumn of 1817.

I have had an interview with your husband, whose sympathy did me both good and harm, for Streicher almost upset my resignation. God alone knows the result! but as I have always assisted my fellow-men when I had the power to do so, I also rely on his mercy to me.

Educate your daughter carefully, that she may make a good wife.

To-day happens to be Sunday; so I will quote you something out of the Bible,--"Love one another." I conclude with best regards to your best of daughters, and with the wish that all your wounds may be healed.

When you visit the ancient ruins [Frau Streicher was in Baden], do not forget that Beethoven has often lingered there; when you stray through the silent pine forests, do not forget that Beethoven often wrote poetry there, or, as it is termed, composed.

246 - To Frau Von Streicher.

How deeply am I indebted to you, my excellent friend, and I have become such a poor creature that I have no means of repaying you. I am very grateful to Streicher for all the trouble he has taken on my behalf [about a house in the Gärtner Strasse], and beg he will continue his inquiries. God will, I hope, one day enable me to return benefit for benefit, but this being at present impossible, grieves me most of all....

Now Heaven be praised! [he thus winds up a long letter about a bad servant,] I have contrived to collect all these particulars for you with no little toil and trouble, and God grant that I may never, never more be obliged to speak, or write, or think again on such a subject, for mud and mire are not more pernicious to artistic soil, than such devilry to any man!!!

247 - To Frau Von Streicher.

As to Frau von Stein [stone], I beg she will not allow Herr von Steiner to turn into stone, that he may still be of service to me; nor must Frau von Stein become too stony towards Herr von Steiner, &c.

My good Frau von Streicher, do not play any trick [Streiche] to your worthy little husband, but rather be to all others Frau von Stein [stone]!!!!

Where are the coverlets for the beds?

248 - To Frau Von Streicher.

... It is now very evident from all this that if you do not kindly superintend things for me, I, with my infirmities, must meet with the same fate as usual at the hands of these people. Their ingratitude towards you is what chiefly degrades both of them in my eyes. But I don't understand your allusion about gossip? on one occasion alone can I remember having forgotten myself for the moment, but with very different people. This is all I can say on the subject. For my part I neither encourage nor listen to the gossip of the lower orders. I have often given you hints on the subject, without telling you a word of what I had heard. Away! away! away! with such things!

249 - To the Archduke Rudolph.

Nussdorf, Sept. 1, 1817.

I hope to be able to join you in Baden; but my invalid condition still continues, and though in some respects improved, my malady is far from being entirely cured. I have had, and still have, recourse to remedies of every kind and shape; I must now give up the long-cherished hope of ever being wholly restored. I hear that Y.R.H. looks wonderfully well, and though many false inferences may be drawn from this as to good health, still every one tells me that Y.R.H. is much better, and in this I feel sincerely interested. I also trust that when Y.R.H. again comes to town, I may assist you in those works dedicated to the Muses. My confidence is placed on Providence, who will vouchsafe to hear my prayer, and one day set me free from all my troubles, for I have served Him faithfully from my childhood, and done good whenever it has been in my power; so my trust is in Him alone, and I feel that the Almighty will not allow me to be utterly crushed by all my manifold trials. I wish Y.R.H. all possible good and prosperity, and shall wait on you the moment you return to town.

[K.]

250 - To G. Del Rio

Vienna, Nov. 12, 1817.

My altered circumstances render it possible that I may not be able to leave Carl under your care beyond the end of this quarter; so, as in duty bound, I give you this warning a quarter in advance. Though it is painful to admit it, my straitened circumstances leave me no choice in the matter; had it been otherwise, how gladly would I have presented you with an additional quarter's payment when I removed Carl, as a slight tribute of my gratitude. I do hope you will believe that such are my genuine and sincere wishes on the subject. If on the other hand I leave Carl with you for the ensuing quarter, commencing in February, I will apprise you of it early in January, 1818. I trust you will grant me this favor, and that I shall not solicit it in vain. If I ever enjoy better health, so that I can earn more money, I shall not fail to evince my gratitude, knowing well how much more you have done for Carl than I had any right to expect; and I can with truth say that to be obliged to confess my inability to requite your services at this moment, distresses me much.

I am, with sincere esteem, your friend,
L. V. BEETHOVEN.

251 - To G. Del Rio.

MY DEAR FRIEND,--

I have been hitherto unable to answer your friendly letter, having been much occupied and still far from well.

As to your proposal, it merits both gratitude and consideration. I must say that the same idea formerly occurred to me about Carl; at this moment, however, I am in the most unsettled state. This was why I made the stipulation to which I begged you to agree, namely, to let you know in the last month of the present quarter whether Carl was to continue with you. In this way our plans would neither be hurried nor demolished. I am, besides, well aware that it can be no advantage to you to have Carl either on his present terms, or according to your last proposal, and on that very account I wished to point out to you in my letter how gladly, besides the usual remuneration, I would have testified my gratitude in some additional manner.

When I spoke of my inability, I knew that his education would cost me even more elsewhere than with you; but what I intended to convey was that every father has a particular object in the education of his child, and it is thus with me and Carl. No doubt we shall soon discover what is best for him; whether to have a tutor here, or to go on as formerly. I do not wish to tie myself down for the moment, but to remain free to act as his interests may dictate.

Carl daily costs me great sacrifices, but I only allude to them on his own account. I know too well the influence his mother contrives to acquire over him, for she seems resolved to show herself well worthy of the name of "Queen of the Night." Besides, she everywhere spreads a report that I do nothing whatever for Carl, whereas she pays everything!! As we have touched on this point, I must thank you for your most considerate letter, which in any event will be of great use to me. Pray ask Herr L.S. to be so kind as to make my excuses to his brother for not having yet called on him. Partly owing to business and also to indisposition, it has been nearly impossible for me to do so. When I think of this oft-discussed affair, I should prefer going to see him on any other subject. She has not applied to me; so it is not my business to promote a meeting between her and her son.

With regard to the other matter, I am told that in this case we must have recourse to compulsion, which will cost me more money, for which I have chiefly to thank Herr Adlersburg [his advocate]. As Carl's education, however, must be carried on so far as possible independent of his mother, for the future as well as the present we must act as I have arranged.

I am, with esteem, your attached friend,
L. V. BEETHOVEN.

252 - To The Archduke Rudolph.

Last day of December, 1817.

The old year has nearly passed away, and a new one draws near. May it bring Y.R.H. no sorrow, but rather may it bestow on you every imaginable felicity! These are my wishes, all concentrated in the one I have just expressed. If it be allowable to speak of myself, I may say that my health is very variable and uncertain. I am unhappily obliged to live at a great distance from Y.R.H., which shall not, however, prevent my having the extreme gratification of waiting on you at the first opportunity. I commend myself to your gracious consideration, though I may not appear to deserve it. May Heaven, for the benefit of so many whom you befriend, enrich each day of your life with an especial blessing! I am always, &c., &c.
[K.]

253 - To G. Del Rio.

Jan. 6, 1818.

To prevent any mistake I take the liberty to inform you that it is finally settled my nephew Carl should leave your excellent institution the end of this month. My hands are also tied with regard to your other proposal, as if I accepted it, my further projects for Carl's benefit would be entirely frustrated; but I sincerely thank you for your kind intentions.

Circumstances may cause me to remove Carl even before the end of the month, and as I may not be here myself, I will appoint some one to fetch him. I mention this to you now, that it may not appear strange when the time comes; and let me add, that my nephew and I shall feel grateful to you through life. I observe that Carl already feels thus, which is to me a proof that although thoughtless, his disposition is not evil; far less has he a bad heart. I am the more disposed to augur well of him from his having been for two years under your admirable guidance.

I am, with esteem, your friend,
L. V. BEETHOVEN.

254 - To G. Del Rio.

Vienna, Jan. 24, 1818.

I do not come to you myself, as it would be a kind of leave-taking, and this I have all my life avoided. Pray accept my heartfelt thanks for the zeal, rectitude, and integrity with which you have conducted the education of my nephew. As soon as I am at all settled, we mean to pay you a visit; but on account of the mother, I am anxious that the fact of my nephew being with me should not be too much known.

I send you my very best wishes, and I beg especially to thank Frau A.Z. for her truly maternal care of Carl.

I am, with sincere esteem, yours,
L. V. BEETHOVEN.

255 - To Czerny.

MY DEAR GOOD KIND CZERNY,--[1]

I have this moment heard that you are in a position I really never suspected; you might certainly place confidence in me, and point out how matters could be made better for you (without any pretensions to patronage on my part). As soon as I have a moment to myself, I must speak to you. Rest assured that I highly value you, and am prepared to prove this at any moment by deeds.

Yours, with sincere esteem,
L. VAN BEETHOVEN.

*[**Note 1:** Zellner, in his Blätter für Musik, relates what follows on Czerny's own authority:--In 1818 Czerny was requested by Beethoven in a letter (which he presented some years ago to Cocks, the London music publisher) to play at one of his last concerts in the large Redoutensaal, his E flat major Concerto, Op. 73. Czerny answered, in accordance with the truth, that having gained his livelihood entirely for many years past by giving lessons on the piano, for more than twelve hours daily, he had so completely laid aside his pianoforte playing, that he could not venture to attempt playing the concerto properly within the course of a few days (which Beethoven desired). On which he received, in the above letter, a touching proof of Beethoven's sympathy. He also learned subsequently that Beethoven had exerted himself to procure him a permanent situation.]*

256 - To F. Ries,--London.

Vienna, March 5, 1818.
MY DEAR RIES,--

In spite of my wishes it was impossible for me to go to London this year [see No. 236]. I beg you will apprise the Philharmonic Society that my feeble health prevented my coming; I trust, however, I shall be entirely restored this spring, so that in the autumn I may avail myself of their offers and fulfil all their conditions.

Pray request Neate, in my name, to make no public use of the various works of mine that he has in his hands, at least not until I come. Whatever he may have to say for himself, I have cause to complain of him.

Potter[1] called on me several times; he seems to be a worthy man, and to have a talent for composition. My wish and hope for you is that your circumstances may daily improve. I cannot, alas! say that such is the case with my own.... I cannot bear to see others want, I must give; you may therefore believe what a loser I am by this affair. I do beg that you will write to me soon. If possible I shall try to get away from this earlier, in the hope of escaping utter ruin, in which case I shall arrive in London by the winter at latest. I know that you will assist an unfortunate friend. If it had only been in my power, and had I not been chained to this place, as I always have been, by circumstances, I certainly would have done far more for you.

Farewell; remember me to Neate, Smart, and Cramer. Although I hear that the latter is a counter subject both to you and to myself, still I rather understand how to manage people of that kind; so notwithstanding all this we shall yet succeed in producing an agreeable harmony in London. I embrace you from my heart. Your friend,

L. VAN BEETHOVEN.

Many handsome compliments to your charming, (and as I hear) handsome wife.

*[**Note 1:** Schindler, in his Biography (Vol. II. 254), states that Cipriani Potter came to Vienna in 1817.]*

257. To The Rechnungsrath, Vincenz Hauschka.[1]

1818.

First and foremost member of our society, and grand cross of the violon--cello! You wish for an heroic subject, whereas I have none but a spiritual one! I am contented; still, I think an infusion of the spiritual would be quite appropriate in such a mass. I have no objections to H. v. Bernard, but you must pay him; I do not speak of myself. As you call yourselves "Friends of Music," it is only natural that you should expect a great deal to be done on the score of friendship.

Now farewell, my good Hauschka! As for myself, I wander about here with music paper, among the hills and dales and valleys, and scribble a great deal to get my daily bread; for I have brought things to such a pass in this mighty and ignominious land of the Goths and Vandals, that in order to gain time for a great composition, I must always previously scrawl away a good deal for the sake of money, to enable me to complete an important work.

However, my health is much improved, and if the matter is urgent, I can do as you wish now.

In haste, your friend,

BEETHOVEN.

*[**Note 1:** Hauschka was at that time on the committee, and agent for the "Friends to Music" who commissioned Beethoven to write an Oratorio in 1815. Schindler is of opinion that the repeated performance of the Abbé Stadler's heroic Oratorio, Die Befreiung von Jerusalem, was the cause of the Society in 1818 bespeaking, through Hauschka, "An oratorio of the heroic order."]*

258 - To The Archduke Rudolph.

1819.

I have the honor to send the masterly variations[1] of Y.R.H. by the copyist Schlemmer, and to-morrow I shall come in person to wait upon Y.R.H., and much rejoice at being able to serve as a companion to my illustrious pupil on the path of fame.

[K.]

*[**Note 1:** The letters 258 and 259, allude to the pianoforte variations composed by the Archduke Rudolph and dedicated to his instructor.]*

259 - To The Archduke Rudolph.

Jan. 1, 1819.

All that can be comprehended in one wish, or individually named,--health, happiness, and prosperity,--all are included in the prayer I offer up for Y.R.H. on this day. May the wish that I also form for myself be graciously accepted by Y.R.H., namely, that I may continue to enjoy the favor of Y.R.H. A dreadful occurrence[1] has lately taken place in my family, which for a long time stunned my senses, and to this must be ascribed my not having waited on Y.R.H., nor taken any notice of the masterly variations of my much-honored and illustrious pupil, and favorite of the Muses. The gratitude I feel for the surprise and the honor you have done me, I dare not venture to express either verbally or in writing, for I am too far beneath you, even if I could or wished ever so ardently to return like for like. May Heaven accept and listen with peculiar favor to my prayers for Y.R.H.'s health. In the course of a few days I trust I shall myself hear the masterpiece Y.R.H. has sent to me, and nothing will rejoice me more than to assist Y.R.H. as early as possible, in taking the place already prepared for you on Parnassus. [K.]

*[**Note 1:** The "dreadful occurrence" which took place in the end of 1818 in Beethoven's family cannot be discovered.]*

260 - To Ries.

Vienna, April [March?] 30, 1819.

DEAR RIES,--

I am only now able to answer your letter of December 18th. Your sympathy does me good. It is impossible for me to go to London at present, being involved here in various ways; but God will, I trust, aid me, and enable me to visit London next winter, when I shall bring the new symphonies with me.

I every day expect the text for a new oratorio, which I am to write for our Musical Society here, and no doubt it will be of use to us in London also. Do what you can on my behalf, for I greatly need it. I should have been glad to receive any commission from the Philharmonic, but Neate's report of the all but failure of the three overtures vexed me much. Each in its own style not only pleased here, but those in E flat major and C major made a profound impression, so that the fate of those works at the Philharmonic is quite incomprehensible to me.

You have no doubt received the arrangement of the Quintet [Op. 104, see No. 238] and the Sonata [Op. 106]. See that both, especially the Quintet, be engraved without loss of time. There is no such hurry about the Sonata, though I should like it to appear within two or three months. Never having received the previous letter to which you allude, I had no scruple in disposing of both works here; but for Germany only. It will be at any rate three months before the Sonata appears here, but you must make haste with the Quintet. As soon as you forward me a check for the money, I will send an authority to the publisher, securing him the exclusive right to these works for England, Scotland, Ireland, France, &c., &c.

You shall receive by the next post the Tempi of the Sonata marked in accordance with Maelzel's metronome. Prince Paul Esterhazy's courier, De Smidt, took the Quintet and the Sonata with him. You shall also have my portrait by the next opportunity, as I understand that you really wish for it.

Farewell! Continue your regard for me,
Your friend,
BEETHOVEN.

All sorts of pretty compliments to your pretty wife!!! From me!!!!

261 - To Ries.

Vienna, April 16, 1819.

DEAR RIES,--

Here are the Tempi of the Sonata.

1st Allegro, Allegro (alone), erase the assai. Maelzel's metronome 𝅗𝅥 = 138.

2d movement, Scherzoso. Maelzel's metronome [𝅗𝅥 = 80.

3d movement, Maelzel's metronome 𝅘𝅥 = 92. Observe that a previous bar is to be inserted here, namely:--

4th movement, Introduzione--largo. Maelzel's metronome 𝅘𝅥𝅯 = 76..

5th and last movement, 3/4 time. Maelzel's metronome 𝅗𝅥=144..

Pray forgive the confused way in which this is written. It would not surprise you if you knew my situation; you would rather marvel that I accomplish so much in spite of it. The Quintet can no longer be delayed, and must shortly appear; but not the Sonata, until I get an answer from you and the check, which I long to see. The name of the courier is De Smidt, by whom you will receive both the Quintet and Sonata. I beg you will give me an immediate answer. I will write more fully next time.

In haste, your
BEETHOVEN.

262 - To Ries.

April 19, 1819.

MY DEAR FRIEND,--

I ask your forgiveness a thousand times for the trouble I cause you. I cannot understand how it is that there are so many mistakes in the copying of the Sonata. This incorrectness no doubt proceeds from my no longer being able to keep a copyist of my own; circumstances have brought this about. May God send me more prosperity, till ---- is in a better position! This will not be for a whole year to come. It is really dreadful the turn affairs have taken, and the reduction of my salary, while no man can tell what the issue is to be till the aforesaid year has elapsed.

If the Sonata be not suitable for London, I could send another, or you might omit the Largo, and begin at once with the Fugue in the last movement, or the first movement, Adagio, and the third the Scherzo, the Largo, and the Allegro risoluto. I leave it to you to settle as you think best. This Sonata was written at a time of great pressure. It is hard to write for the sake of daily bread; and yet I have actually come to this!

We can correspond again about my visit to London. To be rescued from this wretched and miserable condition is my only hope of deliverance, for as it is I can neither enjoy health, nor accomplish what I could do under more favorable auspices.

263 - To The Philharmonic Society In Laibach.[1]

Vienna, May 4, 1819.

I fully appreciate the high compliment paid to me by the respected members of the Philharmonic Society, in acknowledgment of my poor musical deserts, by electing me honorary member of their Society, and sending me the diploma through Herr von Tuscher; and as a proof of my sense of this honor, I intend in due course to forward to the Society an unpublished work of mine.[2] Moreover, at any time when I can be of use to the Society, I shall be prepared to forward their wishes.

I remain,
the humble servant and honorary member
of the Philharmonic Society,
LUDWIG VAN BEETHOVEN.

*[**Note 1:** In Dr. Fr. Keesbacher's pamphlet, "The Philharmonic Society in Laibach, from 1702 to 1862," he says:--"The Philharmonic Society, always anxious to add to its lustre by attracting honorary members, resolved to appoint the great master of harmony as one of these. This idea had previously occurred to them in 1808. At that time they asked Dr. Anton Schmidt whether he thought that the election of Beethoven, and also Hummel's son, would contribute to the advancement of the Society. On that occasion the Society appear to have had recourse to Haydn for the composition of a Canon; whether they applied to him for a new one or an already existing one is not known. Schmidt replied, 'I, for my part, with such an object in view, would prefer giving my vote for the latter, (Hummel's son, who is second Kapellmeister, Haydn being the first, to the reigning Prince Niklas Esterhazy.) Beethoven is as full of caprice as he is devoid of complaisance. I have not seen Father Haydn*

for a long time, his residence being so distant. He is now in failing health and scarcely ever writes; I will, however, shortly call on him and make the attempt to get a Canon from him.' This discouraging picture of Beethoven, who had indeed too often a repulsive manner, might well deprive the Society of all courage to think any more of him as one of their honorary members. On the 15th of March, 1819, however, the Society prepared the diploma for Beethoven, the usually stereotyped form being exceptionally varied in his honor, and running thus:--'The Philharmonic Society here, whose aim it is to promote refinement of feeling and cultivation of taste in the science of music, and who strive by their incessant efforts to impart to the Society both inwardly and outwardly, by the judicious selection of new members, greater value, solidity, and distinction, are universally animated with the desire to see their list adorned by the name of Beethoven. The organ of this society, the undersigned directors, fulfil the general wish in thus performing their most agreeable duty, and giving you, sir, the strongest proof of their profound admiration, by appointing you one of their honorary members.--Laibach, March 15, 1819.'" A facsimile of Beethoven's handwriting is hung up in a frame under glass in the hall of the Society and affixed to Dr. Keesbacher's pamphlet.]

*[**Note 2:** We are told, "One work alone of Beethoven's in the collection of the Society bears visible marks of coming from his own hand, and that is the Pastoral Symphony." The above-mentioned copy is a MS. score (though not in his writing); on the cover is written by himself in red pencil, now almost illegible, "Sinfonie Pastorale;" and underneath are inscribed the following words in ink by another hand: "Beethoven's writing in red pencil." This score contains various corrections in pencil. Two of these appear to be by Beethoven, but unluckily the pencil marks are so much effaced that it is difficult to decide as to the writing. In the scene "By the Rivulet," where the 12/8 time begins (in B flat major), these words are written, "Violoncelli tutti con Basso." The B especially recalls his mode of writing. Moreover the tempo at the beginning of "The Shepherd's Song," (in F, 6/8 time,) allegretto, is qualified by the same hand in pencil thus, Quasi allegro. No direct proof exists of this being sent by him.]*

264 - To F. Ries,--London.

Vienna, May 25, 1819.

... I was at the time burdened with cares beyond all I had ever in my life known,[1] caused solely by my too lavish benefits to others. Do compose industriously! My dear pupil the Archduke Rudolph and I frequently play your works, and he says that my quondam pupil does honor to his master. Now farewell! as I hear that your wife is so handsome, I venture to embrace her in imagination only, though I hope to have that pleasure in person next winter.

Do not forget the Quintet, and the Sonata, and the money, I mean the Honoraire, avec ou sans honneur. I hope soon to hear good news from you, not in allegro time, but veloce prestissimo.

This letter will be given to you by an intelligent Englishman; they are generally very able fellows, with whom I should like to pass some time in their own country.

Prestissimo--Responsio
De suo amico e Maestro,
BEETHOVEN.

*[**Note 1:** In Schindler's Beethoven's Nachlass there is a large calendar of the years 1819 used by Beethoven, in which he has marked, "Arrived at Mödling May 12!!!--miser sum pauper." Carl too was again ill at that time. Beethoven took him to Blöchlinger's Institution, June 22.]*

265 - To the Archduke Rudolph.

1819.

I learned with deep sorrow of your being again unwell; I trust it will only be a passing indisposition. No doubt our very variable spring is the cause of this. I intended to have brought the variations [see No. 259] yesterday; they may well boldly face the light of day, and no doubt Y.R.H. will receive an application for your consent on this point. I very much regret being only able to express a pia desideria for Y.R.H's. health. I earnestly hope the skill of your Aesculapius may at length gain the victory and procure permanent health for Y.R.H.

[K.]

266 - To the Archduke Rudolph.

Mödling, July 15, 1819.

I have been very ill since my last visit to Y.R.H. in town; I hope however to be much better by next week, in which case I will instantly join Y.R.H. at Baden. Meanwhile I went several times to town to consult my physician. My continued distress about my nephew, whose moral character has been almost totally ruined, has been the main cause of my illness. At the beginning of this week I was obliged to resume my guardianship, the other guardian having resigned, and much has taken place for which he has asked my forgiveness. The solicitor has also given up his office, because, having interested himself in the good cause, he has been loudly accused of partiality. Thus these endless perplexities go on, and no help, no consolation! The whole fabric that I had reared now blown away as if by the wind! A pupil of Pestalozzi, at present an inmate of the Institute where I have placed my nephew, seems to think that it will be a difficult matter for him and for my poor Carl to attain any desirable goal. But he is also of opinion that the most advisable step is the removal of my nephew to a foreign country! I hope that the health of Y.R.H., always so interesting to me, leaves nothing to be desired, and I look forward with pleasure to soon being with Y.R.H., that I may be enabled to prove my anxiety to serve you.

[K.]

267 - To the Archduke Rudolph.

1819.

May I beg the favor of Y.R.H. to inform H.R.H. Archduke Ludwig of the following circumstances. Y.R.H. no doubt remembers my mentioning the necessary removal of my nephew from here, on account of his mother. My intention was to present a petition to H.R.H. Archduke Ludwig on the subject; no difficulties however have hitherto arisen on the subject, as all the authorities concerned are in my favor. Among the chief of these are the College of Privy Councillors, the Court of Guardians, and the guardian himself, who all entirely agree with me in thinking that nothing can be more conducive to the welfare of my nephew than being kept at the greatest possible distance from his mother; moreover, all is admirably arranged for the education of my nephew in Landshut, as the estimable and renowned Professor Sailer is to superintend everything connected with the studies of the youth, and I have also some relations there, so no doubt the most desirable results may be thus attained for my nephew. Having, as I already said, as yet encountered no obstacles, I had no wish whatever to trouble H.R.H. the Archduke Ludwig, but I now understand that the mother of my nephew intends to demand an audience from H.R.H. in order to oppose my scheme. She will not scruple to utter all sorts of calumnies against me, but I trust these can be easily refuted by my well known and acknowledged moral character, and I can fearlessly appeal to Y.R.H. for a testimony on this point for the satisfaction of H.R.H. Archduke Ludwig. As for the conduct of the mother of my nephew, it is easily to be inferred from the fact of her having been declared by the Court wholly incapable of undertaking the guardianship of her son. All that she plotted in order to ruin her poor child can only be credited from her own depravity, and thence arises the unanimous agreement about this affair, and the boy being entirely withdrawn from her influence. Such is the natural and unnatural state of the case. I therefore beg Y.R.H. to intercede with H.R.H. Archduke Ludwig, and to warn him against listening to the slanders of the mother, who would plunge her child into an abyss whence he could never be rescued. That sense of justice which guides every party in our just Austrian land, does not entirely exclude her either; at the same time, this very same sense of justice must render all her remonstrances unavailing. A religious view of the Fourth Commandment is what chiefly decides the Court to send away the son as far as possible. The difficulty those must have who conduct the boy's education in not offending against this commandment, and the necessity that the son should never be tempted to fail in this duty or to repudiate it, ought certainly to be taken into consideration. Every effort has been made by forbearance and generosity to amend this unnatural mother, but all has been in vain. If necessary I will supply H.R.H. Archduke Ludwig with a statement on the subject, and, favored by the advocacy of my gracious master Y.R.H. the Archduke Rudolph, I shall certainly obtain justice.

[K.]

268 - To the Archduke Rudolph.

1819.

I regret to say that, owing to a judicial meeting about the affairs of my nephew (being unable to alter the hour fixed), I must give up the pleasure of waiting on Y.R.H. this evening, but shall not fail to do so to-morrow at half-past four o'clock. As for the affair itself, I know that I shall be treated with indulgence. May Heaven at length bring it to a close! for my mind suffers keenly from such a painful turmoil.

[K.]

269 - To the Archduke Rudolph.

Mödling, July 29, 1819.

I heard with deep regret of Y.R.H.'s recent indisposition, and having received no further reliable information on the subject, I am extremely uneasy. I went to Vienna to search in Y.R.H.'s library for what was most suitable to me. The chief object must be to hit off our idea at once, and in accordance with a high class of art, unless the object in view should require different and more practical treatment. On this point the ancient composers offer the best examples, as most of these possess real artistic value (though among them the German Handel and Sebastian Bach can alone lay claim to genius); but freedom and progress are our true aim in the world of art, just as in the great creation at large; and if we moderns are not so far advanced as our forefathers in solidity, still the refinement of our ideas has contributed in many ways to their enlargement. My illustrious musical pupil, himself a competitor for the laurels of fame, must not incur the reproach of onesidedness, et iterum venturus judicare vivos et mortuos. I send you three poems, from which Y.R.H. might select one to set to music. The Austrians have now learned that the spirit of Apollo wakes afresh in the Imperial House; I receive from all sides requests for something of yours. The editor of the "Mode Zeitung" is to write to Y.R.H. on the subject. I only hope that I shall not be accused of being bribed--to be at court and yet no courtier! After that, what is not credible??!!!

I met with some opposition from His Excellency the Obersthofmeister[1] in selecting the music. It is not worth while to trouble Y.R.H. on the subject in writing; but this I will say, that such conduct might have the effect of repelling many talented, good, and noble-minded men, who had not enjoyed the good fortune to learn from personal intercourse with Y.R.H. all the admirable qualities of your mind and heart. I wish Y.R.H. a speedy, speedy recovery, and, for my own peace of mind, that I may hear some good tidings of Y.R.H.

[K.]

*[**Note 1:** Probably the Obersthofmeister, Count Laurencin, by no means approved of the manner in which Beethoven searched for music, which accounts for this outbreak on the part of the irritable maestro.]*

270 - To the Archduke Rudolph.

1819.

I have unhappily only myself to blame! I went out yesterday for the first time, feeling pretty well, but I forgot, or rather paid no attention to the fact, that, being an invalid only just recovering, I ought to have gone home early; I have consequently brought on another attack. I think, however, that by staying at home to-day, all will be right by to-morrow, when I hope to be able to wait on my esteemed and illustrious pupil without fail. I beg Y.R.H. not to forget about Handel's works, as they certainly offer to your mature musical genius the highest nourishment, and their study will always be productive of admiration of this great man.

[K.]

271 - To the Archduke Rudolph.

Mödling, Aug. 31, 1819.

I yesterday received the intelligence of a fresh recognition and homage[1] offered to the admirable qualities of your head and heart. I beg that Y.R.H. will graciously accept my congratulations. They spring from the heart, and do not require to be suggested! I hope things will soon go better with me also. So much annoyance has had a most prejudicial effect on my health, and I am thus far from well; so for some time past I have been obliged to undergo a course of medicine which has only permitted me to devote myself for a few hours in the day to the most cherished boon of Heaven, my art and the Muses. I hope, however, to be able to finish the Mass[2] so that it can be performed on the 19th--if that day is still fixed. I should really be in despair[3] were I prevented by bad health from being ready by that time. I trust, however, that my sincere wishes for the accomplishment of this task may be fulfilled. As to that chef-d'oeuvre, the variations of Y.R.H., I think they should be published under the following title:--

Theme or Subject
composed by L. van Beethoven,
forty times varied,
and dedicated to his Instructor,
by the Illustrious Author.

The inquiries about this work are numerous, and yet, after all, this excellent composition may be ushered into the world in mutilated copies, for Y.R.H. yourself cannot possibly resist giving it first to one person and then to another; so, in Heaven's name, together with the great homage Y.R.H. now publicly receives, let the homage to Apollo (or the Christian Cecilia) also be made public. Perhaps Y.R.H. may accuse me of vanity; but I do assure you that precious as this dedication is to my heart, and truly proud of it as I am, this is certainly not my chief object. Three publishers have offered to take the work,--Artaria, Steiner, and a third whose name does not at this moment occur to me. So of the two I have named, which is to have the variations? I await the commands of Y.R.H. on this point. They are to be engraved at the cost of either of those publishers, according to their own offer. The question now is whether Y.R.H. is satisfied with the title. My idea is that Y.R.H. should entirely close your eyes to the fact of the publication; when it does appear, Y.R.H. may deem it a misfortune, but the world will consider it the reverse. May Providence protect Y.R.H., and shower down the richest blessings of His grace on Y.R.H.'s sacred head, and preserve for me your gracious regard! [On the cover] My indisposition must be my excuse with Y.R.H. for this confused letter.

[K.]

*[**Note 1:** The Emperor Francis had sent the new Archbishop of Olmütz, Archduke Rudolph, the Grand Cross of the Order of St. Stephen.]*

*[**Note 2:** The Mass for the solemnities of the Archduke Rudolph's enthronization in Olmütz (March 20, 1820) was not completed by Beethoven till 1822.]*

*[**Note 3:** Beethoven had, however, no cause for despair on the subject. The kind-hearted Archduke showed the utmost indulgence to him on this occasion as well as on many others, and even at a later period accepted the dedication of this long delayed composition.]*

272 - To the Archduke Rudolph.

[1]
1819.

I perceive that Baron Schweiger has not informed Y.R.H. of the attack I had yesterday. I was suddenly seized with such sharp fever that I entirely lost consciousness; a bruised foot may have contributed to bring this on. It is therefore impossible for me to leave the house to-day. I hope, however, to be quite recovered by to-morrow, and I request Y.R.H. to appoint the orchestra to come to-morrow afternoon at a quarter to three o'clock, that the musicians may appear a little earlier, and leave sufficient time to try over the two Overtures. If Y.R.H. wishes to hear these, I shall require four horns; the Symphonies, however, require only two. For the proper performance of the Symphonies we must have at least four violins, four second, four first, two double basses, two violoncellos. I beg you will be so good as to let me know what you decide on. No pleasure can ever be greater to me than hearing my works performed before my illustrious pupil. May God speedily restore your health, which often causes me anxiety!

[K.]

*[**Note 1:** The letters 272, 273, 274, relate to arrangements for musical meetings at which Beethoven caused his new works to be played for the Archduke.]*

273 - To the Archduke Rudolph.

1819.

I beg you will be so kind as to let Herr von Wranitzky[1] know your commands about the music, and whether to bespeak two or four horns. I have already spoken with him, and suggested his only selecting musicians who can accomplish a performance, rather than a mere rehearsal.

[K.]

*[**Note 1:** Anton Wranitzky (born 1760, died 1819), director of Prince Lobkowitz's opera and band. His brother Paul (born 1756, died 1808) was from 1785 to 1808 Kapellmeister at the Royal Opera in Vienna.]*

274 - To the Archduke Rudolph.

1819.

It is impossible to double the parts by eleven o'clock to-morrow, most of the copyists having so much to write this week. I think therefore you will perhaps appoint next Saturday for our resurrection day, and by that time I expect to be entirely recovered, and better able to conduct, which would have been rather an arduous task for me to-morrow, in spite of my good-will. On Friday I do hope to be able to go out and inquire for Y.R.H.

[K.]

275 - To the Archduke Rudolph.

1819.

(A Fragment.)

The day when a High Mass of mine is performed in honor of the solemnities for Y.R.H. will be the most delightful of my life, and God will enlighten me so that my poor abilities may contribute to the splendors of that solemn occasion. I send you the Sonata with heartfelt gratitude; I think the violoncello part is wanting,--at least I could not lay my hand on it at the moment. As the work is beautifully engraved, I have taken the liberty to add a published copy, and also a violin quintet. In addition to the two pieces written in my hand on Y.R.H.'s name-day, there are two more; the last a grand Fugato, so that it forms one great sonata,[1] which is now shortly to appear, and has been long in my heart dedicated to Y.R.H. The recent occurrence connected with Y.R.H.[2] is not in the slightest degree the cause of this. I beg you will forgive my bad writing. I implore the Lord to bestow His richest blessings on Y.R.H., whose love of humanity is so comprehensive,--one of the choicest of all qualities; and in this respect Y.R.H. will always, either in a worldly or spiritual point of view, be one of our brightest examples.

[K.]

*[**Note 1:** The Grand Sonata with two movements, and two additional ones, of which the last is a grand fugued one, can scarcely be any other than the pianoforte Sonata (Op. 106) composed in 1818, dedicated to the Archduke Rudolph, and published in September, 1819.]*

*[**Note 2:** The "recent occurrence" to which Beethoven alludes is no doubt his being appointed Archbishop.]*

276 - To Herr Blöchlinger

Mödling, Sept. 14, 1819.

85 florins enclosed.

DEAR SIR,--

I have the honor to send you payment for the ensuing month, which begins on the 22d Sept., and I add 10 florins in order to provide for any unforeseen expenses, which you will please account for to me on the 12th October. The following persons alone are to have free access to my nephew: Herr von Bernard, Herr von Oliva, Herr von Piuss.

If any persons, exclusive of those I have named, wish to see my nephew, I will give them a letter to you, when you will be so obliging as to admit them; for the distance to your house is considerable, and those who go there can only do so to oblige me, as, for example, the bandage-maker, &c., &c.

My nephew must never leave your house without a written permission from me. From this you will at once plainly perceive your line of conduct towards Carl's mother. I must impress on you the necessity of these rules (proceeding from the magistrates and myself) being strictly enforced. You, dear sir, are too little experienced in these circumstances, however obvious your other merits are to me, to act on your own judgment in the matter, as you have hitherto done. Credulity can in the present instance only lead to embarrassment, the result of which might prove injurious to you rather than beneficial, and this I wish to avoid for the sake of your own credit.

I hear that my nephew requires, or at all events wishes to have, a variety of things from me; he has only to apply to myself. Be so good as to forward all his letters through Herr Steiner & Co., Pater Noster Gässel, auf'm Graben.

Your obedient
BEETHOVEN,
Sole guardian of my nephew Carl Van Beethoven.

N.B. Any outlay will be at once repaid.

277.

Vienna, Sept. 21, 1819.

In honor of the visit of Herr Schlesinger of Berlin.

L. V. BEETHOVEN.

278 - To Herr Artaria,--Vienna.

Oct. 1, 1819.

MOST EXCELLENT AND MOST VIRTUOUS OF VIRTUOSI, AND NO HUMBUG!

While informing you of all sorts of things from which we hope you will draw the best conclusions, we request you to send us six (say 6) copies of the Sonata in B flat major, and also six copies of the variations on the Scotch songs, as the author's right. We beg you to forward them to Steiner, in Pater Noster Gässel, whence they will be sent to us with some other things.

In the hope that you are conducting yourself with all due propriety and decorum, we are your, &c.,

B----.

279 - A Sketch Written by Beethoven,--

Corrected by Artaria's Bookkeeper, Wuister.

1819.

Having heard from Herr B. that Y.R. Highness [the Archduke Rudolph] has written a most masterly work, we wish to be the first to have the great honor

of publishing Y.R. Highness's composition, that the world may become acquainted with the admirable talents of so illustrious a Prince. We trust Y. Royal Highness will comply with our respectful solicitation.
FALSTAFF--[1]
Ragged Rascal!

*[**Note 1:** The name Beethoven gave to Artaria's partner, Bolderini.]*

280 - To Artaria.

Mödling, Oct. 12, 1819.

Pray forgive me, dear A. (?), for plaguing you as follows:--

We are coming to town the day after to-morrow, and expect to arrive at four o'clock. The two days' festival compels us to return the same day, as Carl must prepare with his master here for the second examination, these very holidays enabling the tutor to devote more time to him; but I must soon return to town on account of the certificate of Carl's birth, which costs more time and money than I like. I at all times dislike travelling by the diligence, and this one has moreover one peculiarity, that you may wish to go on what day you please, but it always turns out to be a Friday on which it sets off; and though a good Christian, still one Friday in the year is sufficient for me. I beg you will request the leader of the choir (the devil alone knows what the office is!) to be so good as to give us Carl's certificate of birth on the afternoon of the same day if possible. He might do so at seven o'clock in the morning, at the time we arrive; but he ought to be punctual, for Carl is to appear at the examination at half-past seven o'clock. So it must be either to-morrow at seven, or at all events in the afternoon. We shall call on you to-morrow before seven o'clock to inquire about this, with the proviso of a visit later in the day. In haste, and asking your pardon,
Your
L. VAN BEETHOVEN.

281 - Petition to the Magistracy.[1]

Oct. 30, 1819.

GENTLEMEN,--
My brother, Carl van Beethoven, died on November 5, 1815, leaving a boy twelve years old,--his son Carl. In his will, by clause 5, he bequeathed to me the guardianship of the boy, and in the codicil B he expressed a wish that his widow, Johanna, should have a share in this duty, adding that, for the sake of his child, he recommended her to submit to my guidance. This explicit declaration of the father, added to my legal claim, I being the nearest relative (clause 198), entitles me clearly to the guardianship of my nephew, Carl van

Beethoven; and the Court of Justice, by their Decree E, committed to me, under existing circumstances, the guardianship, to the exclusion moreover of Beethoven's widow. A journey on business having compelled me to be for some time absent, I did not object to an official guardian supplying my place for the time, which was effected by the nomination of the Town Sequestrator, Herr Nussböck.

Being now, however, finally settled here, and the welfare of the boy very precious to me, both love and duty demand that I should resume my rights; especially as this talented lad is coming to an age when greater care and expense must be bestowed on his education, on which his whole future prospects depend. This duty ought not to be confided to any woman, far less to his mother, who possesses neither the will nor the power to adopt those measures indispensable to a manly and suitable education.

I am the more anxious to reclaim my guardianship of Carl, as I understand that, in consequence of want of means to defray the expenses of the school where I placed him, he is to be removed, and his mother wishes him to live with her, in order herself to spend his trifling provision, and thus save the one half of her pension, which, according to the decree, she is bound to apply to his use.

I have hitherto taken a paternal charge of my nephew, and I intend to do the same in future at my own expense, being resolved that the hopes of his deceased father, and the expectations I have formed for this clever boy, shall be fulfilled by his becoming an able man and a good citizen.

With this view I accordingly request that the highly respected magistrates whom I now address will be pleased to annul the Town Sequestrator Nussböck's interim office, and forthwith transfer to me the sole guardianship of my nephew Carl van Beethoven.[2]

LUDWIG VAN BEETHOVEN.

*[**Note 1:** Evidently drawn up by his advocate, Dr. Bach, from Beethoven's notes.]*
*[**Note 2:** The magisterial decree of Nov. 4, 1819, was adverse to Beethoven.]*

282 - To F. Ries,--London.

Vienna, Nov. 10, 1819.
DEAR RIES,--

I write to let you know that the Sonata is already out, though only a fortnight ago, and it is nearly six months since I sent you both the Quintet and the Sonata. In the course of a few days I will send them both to you engraved, and from them you can correct the two works.

Having received no letter from you on the subject, I thought the thing was at an end. I have indeed made shipwreck already with Neate this year! I only wish you could contrive to get me the fifty ducats which I have yet to receive, as I calculated on them, and really am in great want of money. I shall say no more to-day, but must inform you that I have nearly completed a new Grand Mass. Write to me whether you could do anything with this in London; but soon, very soon, and send the money soon also for both works. I will write more fully next time. In haste,

Your true and faithful friend,

BEETHOVEN.

283 - To the Archduke Rudolph.

Dec. 14, 1819.

Immediately on last leaving Y.R.H. I was taken ill, of which I apprised Y.R.H., but owing to a change in my household, neither the letter in question nor another to Y.R.H. was ever sent. In it I begged Y.R.H.'s indulgence, having some works on hand that I was obliged to dispatch with all speed, owing to which I was, alas! compelled to lay aside the Mass also.[1] I hope Y.R.H. will ascribe the delay solely to the pressure of circumstances. This is not the time to enter fully into the subject, but I must do so as soon as the right moment arrives, that Y.R.H. may not form too severe or undeserved a judgment of me. My heart is always with Y.R.H., and I trust at length circumstances may in so far change, that I may be able to contribute more than I have hitherto done, to perfecting your great talent. I think, however, Y.R.H. is already aware of my good-will in this respect, and is fully convinced that insurmountable obstacles alone can ever detain me from the most excellent of all princes, so revered by me, and so entwined with every feeling of my heart. I did not till yesterday hear of the mistake about the two letters, and I now intend to bring them myself, for I have no one in my service on whom I can depend. I will present myself at your house this afternoon at half-past four o'clock. My warmest thanks for Y.R.H.'s kind letter to me. When Y.R.H. thus vouchsafes to declare your esteem for me, it only heightens and increases my impulse to all that is good.

*[**Note 1:** Another allusion to the Grand Mass in D, which seemed likely never to be completed.]*

284 - Memorandum.

1822.

The Mass[1] will soon be all in Y.R.H.'s hands; it ought to have been, and would have been so long ago, but--but--but--when Y.R.H. becomes acquainted with my circumstances, you will be surprised that I have even now been able to finish it.

[K.]

*[**Note 1:** The circumstances which prevented the completion of this work were undoubtedly his perpetual state of strife with his nephew and his sister-in-law.]*

285 - To the Archduke Rudolph.

I heard with heartfelt sorrow of Y.R.H.'s indisposition, but hope soon to hear of your recovery. Why am I also ill? for I might possibly discover the best mode of restoring Y.R.H. I will call again to inquire after Y.R.H., and hope to hear good news. [K.]

286 - To the Archduke Rudolph.

I have been rather an invalid all this time, though I try to think myself tolerably well. I deeply regret to hear of Y.R.H.'s attack, especially as I knew nothing of it, or I certainly should have hastened to inquire whether it was in my power in any way to alleviate your sufferings. To-morrow, in compliance with Y.R.H.'s wish, I shall certainly enjoy the pleasure of seeing my own most dear and illustrious master. [K.]

287 - To the Royal and Imperial High Court of Appeal.

Jan. 7, 1820.

GENTLEMEN,--

On the plea of the Decree A, I sought to have transferred to myself the guardianship of my nephew, Carl v. Beethoven, but was referred by the magistracy to the previous decision. On my consequent remonstrance the same result ensued.

I find myself the more aggrieved by this, inasmuch as not only are my own rights set at naught, but even the welfare of my nephew is thus utterly disregarded. I am therefore compelled to have recourse to the highest Court of Appeal to lay before them my well-founded claim, and rightfully to demand that the guardianship of my nephew should be restored to me.

My reasons are the following:--

1st. I am entitled to the guardianship of my nephew, not only by his father's will, but by law, and this the Court of Justice confirmed to the exclusion of the mother. When business called me away from Vienna, I conceded that Herr Nussböck should act for me ad interim. Having now, however, taken up my residence here, the welfare of my nephew demands that I should again undertake the office of his guardian.

2d. My nephew has arrived at an age when he requires to be trained to a higher degree of cultivation. Neither his mother nor his present guardian are calculated to guide the boy in the pursuit of his studies. The former, in the first place, because she is a woman; and as to her conduct, it has been legally proved that, to say the least of it, she has no creditable testimonials to bring forward,[1] on which account she was expressly prohibited from acting by the Court of Justice. How the Honorable Magistracy could nevertheless again appoint her is quite incomprehensible. The latter is unfit; because, on the one hand, his office as sequestrator and administrator of houses and lands, occupies his time too much to enable him properly to undertake the duties of guardian to the boy; and, on the other, because his previous occupation as a paper manufacturer, does not inspire me with any confidence that he possesses the intelligence or judgment indispensable to conduct a scientific education.

3d. The welfare of my nephew is dearer to my heart than it can be to any one else. I am myself childless, and have no relations except this boy, who is full of talent, and I have good grounds to hope the best for him, if properly trained. Now I am compelled to hear that he has been delayed a whole year by remaining in his previous class, from want of means to defray the expense, and that his mother intends to remove him from his present school, and wishes him to live with her. What a misfortune to the boy, were he to become a victim to the mismanagement of his mother, who would fain squander on herself that portion of her pension which she is obliged to devote to the education of her son!

I have therefore declared in due form to the Honorable Magistracy that I am myself willing to undertake the expenses of his present school, and also to provide the various masters required. Being rather deaf, which is an impediment to conversation, I have requested the aid of a colleague, and suggested for this purpose Herr Peters, Councillor of Prince Lobkowitz, in order that a person may forthwith be appointed to superintend the education and progress of my nephew, that his moral character may one day command esteem, and whose acquirements may be a sure guaranty to all those who feel an interest in the youth's welfare, that he will undoubtedly receive the education and culture necessary to develop his abilities.

My efforts and wishes have no other aim than to give the boy the best possible education,--his abilities justifying the brightest hopes,--and to fulfil the trust placed in my brotherly love by his father. The shoot is still flexible; but if longer neglected it will become crooked, and outgrow the gardener's training hand, and upright bearing, intellect, and character, be destroyed forever.

I know no duty more sacred than the education and training of a child. The chief duties of a guardian consist in knowing how to appreciate what is good, and in adopting a right course; then alone has proper attention been devoted to the welfare of his ward, whereas in opposing what is good he neglects his duty.

Indeed, keeping in view what is most for the benefit of the boy, I do not object to the mother in so far sharing in the duties of a guardian that she may visit her son, and see him, and be apprised of all the measures adopted for his education; but to intrust her with the sole guardianship of the boy without a strict guardian by her side, would cause the irrevocable ruin of her son.

On these cogent grounds I reiterate my well-founded solicitation, and feel the more confident of a favorable answer, as the welfare of my nephew alone guides my steps in this affair.[2]

*[**Note 1:** Schindler states that during these law proceedings the widow of Beethoven's brother had another child.]*

*[**Note 2:** The Court excluded Carl's mother from all share in his education, and from all direct influence over her son, and again restored to Beethoven the full authority of a guardian.]*

288 - To His Highness the Archduke Rudolph.

From your obedient servant,
L. V. BEETHOVEN.

Jan. 12, 1820.

289 - Testimonial in Favor of Herr V. Kandeler.

It is certainly the duty of every musical composer to become acquainted with all the earlier as well as more modern poets, in order to select what is most suitable to his purpose for songs. Such, however, not being invariably the case, this present collection of Herr v. Kandeler's cannot fail to be useful and commendable to many who wish to write songs, and also tend to induce more able poets to contribute something in the same direction.

LUDWIG V. BEETHOVEN.--M.P.
I entirely agree with Herr v. Beethoven.
JOS. WEIGEL.

290 - To Theodore Amadeus Hoffmann.[1]

Vienna, March 23, 1820.

I seize the opportunity through Herr N. of approaching a man so gifted as yourself. You have also written of my humble self, and Herr N.N. showed me some lines of yours about me in his album; I have, therefore, every reason to believe that you feel some interest in me. Permit me to say that, on the part of so talented a man as yourself, this is truly gratifying to me. I wish you all possible good and happiness, and remain,
Sir, with esteem, your obedient
BEETHOVEN.

*[**Note 1:** It is well known that Hoffmann, in the years 1809 to 1812, wrote the first really important articles on Beethoven's works for the Leipzig A.M. Zeitung on his instrumental music, his trios, and masses, &c., &c.]*

291 - To Herr Haslinger,--Adjutanterl.

I request the Adjutant to lend me the score of the Overture in E flat, which I will return as soon as the performance is over. I also beg he will be so good as to send me Kirnberger's work to supply the place of mine, as I am at this moment giving lessons in counterpoint, and have been unable to find my own manuscript amid my confused mass of papers. Yours,
MI CONTRA FA.

292 - To Tobias,--Adjutant.

MOST WORTHY ADJUTANT,--

I have made a bet of ten florins, W.W., against the truth of your having been obliged to pay a compensation of 2000 florins to Artaria for the new edition of Mozart's works, which have been again and again engraved and sold everywhere. I really wish to know the truth on this subject, for I cannot possibly believe what is said. If it be the fact that you have been so unhandsomely treated, then Ah, dolce contento must pay the ten florins. Send me a true report. Farewell; be a good Christian. Your

BEETHOVEN.

293 - To the Archduke Rudolph.

Vienna, April 3, 1820.

YOUR ROYAL HIGHNESS,--

So far as I can recollect, when I was about to wait on you, I was told that Y.R.H. was indisposed; I called on Sunday evening to inquire, having been assured that Y.R.H. did not intend to set off on Monday. In accordance with my usual custom, not to remain long in an anteroom, I hurried away after receiving this information, though I observed that the gentleman in waiting wished to say something to me. Unhappily I did not hear till Monday afternoon that Y.R.H. had really gone to Olmütz. I must confess that this caused me a very painful feeling, but my consciousness of never having neglected my duty in any respect, induced me to suppose that the same may have been the case on this occasion, as it often is in human life,--for I can easily conceive that Y.R.H., immersed in ceremonies and novel impressions, had very little time to spare in Olmütz for other things. I should otherwise certainly have anticipated Y.R.H. in writing. May I ask you graciously to inform me what length of stay you intend to make in Olmütz? It was reported that Y.R.H. intended to return here towards the end of May; but a few days ago I heard that you were to remain a year and a half in Olmütz; owing to this I may perhaps have adopted wrong measures, not with regard to Y.R.H., but myself. As soon as I receive information from you on the subject, I will enter into further explanations. May I also beg that in the mean time Y.R.H. will not listen to certain reports about me? I have heard a great deal of what may be termed gossip here, which people seem to think may be acceptable to Y.R.H. As Y.R.H. is pleased to say that I am one of those whom you esteem, I can confidently declare that Y.R.H. is the person whom I value most in the universe. Although no courtier, I believe that Y.R.H. knows me too thoroughly to believe that mere selfish interest has ever attached or attracted me towards Y.R.H., but, on the contrary, true and heartfelt affection alone. I can with truth say that a second Blondel has long since set forth on his pilgrimage, and if no Richard can be found in this world for me, God shall be my Sovereign!

It seems to me that my idea of giving a quartet is the best; even though some works have been already performed on a grand scale at Olmütz, still something might thus be introduced into Moravia to attract the attention of the musical world, and for the benefit of Art.

If, according to the above reports, Y.R.H. should return here in May, I advise Y.R.H. to reserve your spiritual children for me [see No. 279] till then, because it would be better that I should hear them performed by yourself. But if your stay in Olmütz is really to be of such long duration, I will receive them now with the greatest pleasure, and strive to accompany Y.R.H. to the summit of Parnassus. May God preserve Y.R.H. in health for the good of humanity, and also for that of all your warm admirers. I beg you will be graciously pleased soon to write to me. Y.R.H. cannot fail to be convinced of my readiness at all times to fulfil your wishes.

I am Y.R.H.'s humble and faithful servant,

LUDWIG V. BEETHOVEN

294 - To the Archduke Rudolph.

Mödling, Aug. 3, 1820.

I have this moment received the letter in which Y.R.H. informs me yourself of your journey hither, and I sincerely thank Y.R.H. for such a mark of attention. I intended to have hastened to town to-morrow to wait on Y.R.H., but no carriage is to be had; I expect however to get one before next Saturday, when I shall lose no time, and set off at an early hour to inquire for Y.R.H. With regard to the sacrifice Y.R.H. intends to offer up to the Muses, I will make a proposal verbally on the subject. I heartily rejoice in knowing that Y.R.H. is once more so near me. May I in all respects be enabled to assist in fulfilling your wishes! May Heaven bless Y.R.H., and mature all your plans!

[K.]

295 - To Herr Artaria, Falstaff, & Co.

Vienna, Oct. 26, 1820.

I politely request that you will hand over to Herr Oliva the sum of 300 florins, which has no doubt already been received by you in full. Having been entirely occupied by removing to my new lodgings, I could not do myself the honor of expressing my thanks to you and Sir John Falstaff in person.

Your obedient servant,

LUDWIG V. BEETHOVEN.

296 - To Bolderini.

MY VERY WORTHY FALSTAFF!--

I request, with all due civility, that you will send me a copy of each of the two works for pianoforte and flute, with variations. As for the receipt, you shall have it to-morrow; and I also beg you will forward it forthwith. Give my compliments to Herr Artaria, and thank him from me for his kind offer of an advance, but as I have received from abroad the money due to me, I do not require to avail myself of his aid. Farewell, Knight Falstaff; do not be too dissipated, read the Gospel, and be converted!

We remain, your well-affected

BEETHOVEN.

To Sir John Falstaff, Knight.

To the care of Herr Artaria & Co.

297 - To the Archduke Rudolph.

Mödling, Sept. 1820.

Since last Tuesday evening I have been far from well, but hoped by Friday, certainly, to have had the happiness of waiting on Y.R.H. This proved a delusion, and it is only to-day that I am able to say confidently that I expect to present myself before Y.R.H. next Monday or Tuesday at an early hour. I ascribe my illness to having taken an open calèche, in order not to miss my appointment with Y.R.H. The day was very wet and positively cold here towards the evening. Nature seems almost to have been offended by the liberty I took, and by my audacity, and to have punished me in consequence. May Heaven bestow on Y.R.H. all that is good and holy, as well as every charm and blessing, and on me your favor, but only in so far as justice sanctions!

[K.]

298 - To Herr Artaria & Co.

Vienna, Dec. 17, 1820.

I thank you warmly for the advance of 150 florins, for which I have made out the receipt in the name of his Imperial Highness the Cardinal, and I beg, as I am in danger of losing one of my bank shares, that you will advance me another 150 florins, which I pledge myself to repay within three months at latest from this date. As a proof of my gratitude, I engage in this letter to make over to you, as your exclusive property, one of my compositions, consisting of two or more movements, without claiming payment for it hereafter.

Your ever-complaisant
BEETHOVEN.
[L.S.]

299 - To Tobias V. Haslinger.

Baden, Sept. 10, 1821.
MY VERY DEAR FRIEND,--

On my way to Vienna yesterday, sleep overtook me in my carriage, which was by no means strange, for having been obliged to rise so early every morning, I never had a good night's sleep. While thus slumbering I dreamt that I had gone on a far journey, to no less a place than to Syria, on to Judea, and back, and then all the way to Arabia, when at length I actually arrived at Jerusalem. The Holy City gave rise to thoughts of the Holy Books. No wonder then if the man Tobias occurred to me, which also naturally led me to think of our own little Tobias and our great Tobias. Now during my dream-journey, the following Canon came into my head:--

But scarcely did I wake when away flew the Canon, and I could not recall any part of it. On returning here however, next day, in the same carriage, (that of a poor Austrian musician,) I resumed my dream-journey, being, however, on this occasion wide awake, when lo and behold! in accordance with the laws of the association of ideas the same Canon again flashed across me; so being now awake I held it as fast as Menelaus did Proteus, only permitting it to be changed into three parts.

Farewell! I intend to send next something composed on Steiner's name, to show that his is no heart of stone [Stein]. Adieu, my good friend; it is my most heartfelt wish that you may prosper as a publisher; may all credit be given to you, and yet may you never require credit. Sing daily the Epistles of St. Paul, and daily visit Father Werner, who can show you in his little book how to go straight to heaven. See, how anxious I am about the welfare of your soul!

I remain always, with infinite pleasure, henceforth and forever,

Your faithful debtor,
BEETHOVEN.

300 - To the Archduke Rudolph.

Unterdöbling, July 18, 1821.

I yesterday heard of Y.R.H.'s arrival here; joyful tidings for me, but saddened by knowing that it must be some time before I can have the good fortune to wait on Y.R.H.; having been long very ill, at last jaundice declared itself, which I consider a most loathsome malady. I trust, however, I shall be so far recovered as to see Y.R.H. before you leave this. Last winter, too, I had some very severe rheumatic attacks. Much of this proceeds from the melancholy state of my family affairs; I have hitherto hoped, by every possible exertion on my part, at last to remedy these. That Providence, who searches my inmost heart, and knows that as a man I have striven sacredly to fulfil all the duties imposed on me by humanity, God, and Nature, will no doubt one day extricate me from all these troubles. The Mass [in D] will be delivered to Y.R.H. here. I hope Y.R.H. will excuse my entering into the various causes of the delay. The details could not be otherwise than painful to Y.R.H. I would often gladly have written to Y.R.H. from here, but you told me to wait till I first heard from you. What, then, was I to do? Y.R.H. might have been displeased had I not attended to your injunction, and I know that there are people who are glad to calumniate me to Y.R.H., which pains me exceedingly. I therefore often think that my sole recourse is to keep quiet till Y.R.H. expresses a wish either to see or to hear of me. I was told that Y.R.H. had been indisposed, but I hope it was nothing serious. May Heaven shower down its most precious blessings on Y.R.H.! I trust it may not be very long before I shall be so fortunate as to assure Y.R.H. how entirely I am, &c., &c.

[K.]

301 - To the Archduke Rudolph.

Unterdöbling, July 18, 1821.

I have written a long and minute letter to Y.R.H., which my copyist Schlemmer will deliver. I wrote it on hearing the day before yesterday of the arrival of Y.R.H. How much I grieve that the attack of jaundice with which I am affected prevents my at once hastening to Y.R.H. to express in person my joy at your arrival. May the Lord of all things, for the sake of so many others, take Y.R.H. under His protection!

[K.]

302 - To the Most Celebrated Music Firm in Europe, Messrs. Steiner & Co., Paternoster-(Miserere) Gässel.

I request Geh'-bauer[1] to send me two tickets, as some of my friends wish to attend your hole-and-corner music. You probably have some of these worthless admission tickets; so let me have one or two.

The part I send belongs to the Chorus, of which Bauer has the other portions. Your amicus

BEETHOVEN.

*[**Note 1:** Gebauer established the "Concerts Spirituels" in 1819, and died in 1822.]*

303 - Address Unknown.

Baden, Sept. 27, 1821.

I hope, sir, that you will forgive the liberty I take in thus intruding on you. The bearer of this, H. v.----, has been commissioned by me to exchange or sell a bank-note. Being ignorant of everything connected with these matters, I beg you will be so good as to communicate your views and advice to the bearer. The two illnesses I had last winter and summer rather deranged all my calculations. I have been here since the 7th of September, and must remain till the end of October. All this costs a great deal of money, and prevents my earning it as usual. I indeed expect shortly to receive money from abroad, but as bank-notes stand so high at present, I consider this the easiest resource, and intend subsequently to purchase a new bank-note in its place.

Immediate--in haste.
Your friend,
BEETHOVEN.

[This unsealed letter was enclosed in an envelope on which was written:]

You will at once see what kind of commercial genius I am. After writing the enclosed, I for the first time consulted a friend about the note, who pointed out to me that all I had to do was to cut off a coupon, and the affair was completed. I rejoice, therefore, not to be obliged to plague you further on the subject.

Yours,
BEETHOVEN.

304 - To the Archduke Rudolph.

Feb. 27, 1822.

I went to-day early to the Palace, not, indeed, with the intention of meeting Y.R.H., (not being yet dressed), but only to beg Zips to mention that I had called, and was sincerely rejoiced at your arrival here; but I could no longer discover Y.R.H.'s apartments, and wherever I knocked in the hope of finding Y.R.H., my dress seemed to be so closely scrutinized that I hurried away, and write to-day to recommend myself to Y.R.H. To-morrow I intend to pay my respects to Y.R.H., when I hope also to hear whether the usual musical and intellectual meetings are to continue, and when they are to take place. My not having written all this time to Y.R.H. has indeed a very bad appearance, but I delayed from day to day, hoping always to send the Mass, the mistakes in which were really quite dreadful; so much so that I was obliged to revise every part, and thus the delay occurred. Other pressing occupations and various circumstances tended to impede me, which is often the case when a man least expects it. That Y.R.H., however, was ever present with me is shown by the following copies of some novelties,[1] which have been lying finished by me for some time for Y.R.H., but I resolved not to forward them till I could at the same time send the Mass. The latter now only requires binding, when it shall be respectfully delivered to Y.R.H. by myself. Sincerely rejoiced at the hope of soon personally waiting on Y.R.H., I remain, with devoted homage, yours till death.

[K.]
[Note 1: The novelties which Beethoven sends to the Archduke are:--

Six bagatelles for the pianoforte, Op. 126 (composed in 1821).
Sonata for pianoforte in E major " 109 (" " ?1821).
" " " A flat major " 110 (" " 1821).]

305 - To F. Ries,--London.

Vienna, April 6, 1822.

MY DEAREST AND BEST RIES,--

Having been again in bad health during the last ten months, I have hitherto been unable to answer your letter. I duly received the 26l. sterling, and thank you sincerely; I have not, however, yet got the sonata you dedicated to me. My greatest work is a Grand Mass that I have recently written. As time presses, I can only say what is most urgent. What would the Philharmonic give me for a symphony?

I still cherish the hope of going to London next spring, if my health admits of it! You will find in me one who can thoroughly appreciate my dear pupil, now become a great master, and who can tell what benefit art might derive from our conjunction! I am, as ever, wholly devoted to my Muse, who constitutes the sole happiness of my life, and I toil and act for others as I best can. You have two children; I only one (my brother's son); but you are married, so both yours will not cost you so much as my one costs me.

Now farewell! kiss your handsome wife for me until I can perform this solemn act in person.

Your attached
BEETHOVEN.

Pray send me your dedication, that I may strive to return the compliment, which I mean to do as soon as I receive your work.

306 - To Herren Peters & Co., Music Publishers,--Leipzig.

Vienna, June 5, 1822.

GENTLEMEN,--

You did me the honor to address a letter to me at a time when I was much occupied, and I have also been extremely unwell for the last five months. I now only reply to the principal points. Although I met Steiner by chance a few days ago, and asked him jestingly what he had brought me from Leipzig, he did not make the smallest allusion to your commission or to yourself. He urged me, however, in the very strongest manner, to pledge myself to give him the exclusive right of publishing all my works, both present and future,--and indeed to sign a contract to that effect,--which I declined. This trait sufficiently proves to you why I often give the preference to other publishers both home and foreign. I love uprightness and integrity, and am of opinion that no one should drive a hard bargain with artists, for, alas! however brilliant the exterior of Fame may appear, an artist does not enjoy the privilege of being the daily guest of Jupiter on Olympus; unhappily commonplace humanity only too often unpleasantly drags him down from these pure ethereal heights.

The greatest work I have hitherto written is a Grand Mass with Choruses, and four obbligati voice parts, and full orchestra. Several persons have applied to me for this work, and I have been offered 100 Louis d'or, hard cash, for it; but I demand at least 1000 florins C.M. [20 florins to the mark], for which sum I will also furnish a pianoforte arrangement. Variations on a waltz [Diabelli's] for the piano (they are numerous), 30 ducats in gold,--N.B. Vienna ducats. With regard to songs, I have several rather important descriptive ones: as, for example, a comic Aria, with full orchestra, on Goethe's text, "Mit Mädeln sich vertragen;" and another Aria, in the same style, 16 ducats each (furnishing also a pianoforte arrangement if required); also several descriptive songs, with pianoforte accompaniment, 12 ducats each; among these is a little Italian Cantata, with Recitative; there is also a Song with recitative among the German ones. A Song with pianoforte accompaniment, 8 ducats. An Elegy, four voices, with the accompaniment of two violins, viola, and violoncello, 24 ducats. A Dervise Chorus, with full orchestra, 20 ducats.

Also the following instrumental music: a Grand March for full orchestra, with pianoforte accompaniment, 12 ducats, written for the tragedy of "Tarpeia." Romance for the violin (a solo with full orchestra), 15 ducats. Grand Terzet for two oboes, and one English horn (which might be arranged for other instruments), 30 ducats. Four military Marches with Turkish music; when applied for, I will name the sum. Bagatelles, or minor pianoforte solos, the price to be fixed when required. The above works are all completed. Solo pianoforte Sonata, 40 ducats (which could soon be delivered); Quartet for two violins, tenor, and violoncello, 50 ducats (this will also soon be ready). I am by no means so anxious about these, however, as about a full and complete edition of my works, being desirous to edit them during my lifetime. I have indeed received many proposals on this subject, but accompanied by stipulations to which I could scarcely agree, and which I neither could nor would fulfil. I am willing to undertake, in the course of two years, or possibly a year, or a year and a half, with proper assistance, to edit and superintend a complete edition of my works, and to furnish a new composition in each style; namely, a new work in the style of variations, one in the sonata style, and so on in every separate class of work that I have ever composed, and for the whole combined I ask 10,000 florins C.M.

I am no man of business, and only wish I were; as it is, I am guided by the offers made to me by different competitors for my works, and such a competition is rather strong just now. I request you to say nothing on the subject, because, as you may perceive from the proceedings of these gentlemen, I am exposed to a great deal of annoyance. When once my works appear published by you, I shall no longer be plagued. I shall be very glad if a connection be established between us, having heard you so well spoken of. You will then also find that I infinitely prefer dealing with one person of your description than with a variety of people of the ordinary stamp.

Pray, let me have an immediate answer, as I am now on the verge of deciding on the publication of various works. If you consider it worth while, be so good as to send me a duplicate of the list with which you furnished Herr Steiner. In the expectation of a speedy reply, I remain, with esteem,

Your obedient

LUDWIG VAN BEETHOVEN.

307 - To Herren Peters & Co.

Vienna, July 26, 1822.

I write merely to say that I agree to give you the Mass and pianoforte arrangement of it for 1000 florins C.M. You shall receive the above, written out in score, by the end of July, perhaps a few days sooner or later. As I am always very much occupied, and have been indisposed for the last five months, and works to be sent to a distance requiring the most careful supervision, I must proceed rather more slowly than usual. At all events, Steiner shall get nothing further from me, as he has just played me a most Jewish trick; so he is not one of those who might have had the Mass. The competition for my works is at present very great, for which I thank the Almighty, as I have hitherto been such a loser. I am the foster-father of my brother's destitute child, a boy who shows so much aptitude for scientific pursuits that not only does his study of these, and his maintenance, cost a great deal of money, but I must also strive to make some future provision for him; being neither Indians nor Iroquois, who, as we know, leave everything to Providence, whereas we consider a pauper's existence to be a very sad one.

I assure you on my honor, which, next to God, is what I prize most, that I authorized no one to accept commissions for me. My fixed principle has always been never to make any offer to publishers; not from pride, but simply from a wish to ascertain how far the empire of my small talents extended.

I must conclude for to-day, and wishing you every success, I am, with esteem,

Your obedient
BEETHOVEN.

308 - To Herr Peters.

[1]
Vienna, August 3, 1822.

I already wrote to you that my health was still far from being quite restored. I am obliged to have recourse to baths and mineral waters as well as to medicine; all this makes me rather unpunctual, especially as I must go on writing; corrections, too, run away with a great deal of time.

As to the songs and marches and other trifles, my choice is still undecided, but by the 15th of this month everything shall be ready to be sent off. I await your orders on the subject, and in the mean time shall make no use of your bill of exchange. As soon as I know that the money for the Mass and the other works has arrived here, all shall be ready for delivery by the 15th; and after that date I must set off to some mineral waters near this, when it will be most desirable for me to avoid all business for a time. More as to other matters when less occupied. Pray, do not suspect me of any ignoble motives. It pains me when I am obliged to bargain.

In haste. With esteem, yours,
BEETHOVEN.

*[**Note 1:** Schindler states that the advance of 360 florins C.M. was made to Beethoven in August, 1822. The receipt is dated Nov. 30, 1825.]*

309 - To Herr Artaria.

August 22, 1822.

Being overwhelmed with work, I can only briefly say that I will always do what I can to repay your obliging kindness to me. With regard to the Mass, I have been offered 1000 florins (C.M.) for it. My circumstances do not permit me to accept a less sum from you; all that I can do is to give you the preference. Rest assured that I do not ask you one farthing more than others have offered me, which I can prove to you by written documents. You can consider about this, but I must request you to send me an answer on the subject tomorrow, it being a post-day, and my decision expected elsewhere. With regard to the 150 florins for which I am your debtor, I intend to make you a proposal, as I stand in great need of the 1000 florins.

I beg you will observe strict secrecy as to the Mass. Now, as ever,

Your grateful friend,
BEETHOVEN.

310 - To Herr Peters,--Leipzig

Vienna, November 22, 1822.

I now reply to your letter of the 9th November, in which I expected to find just reproaches for my apparent negligence, you having sent me the money and as yet received nothing in return. Unfair as this may appear, I know you would be mollified towards me in a few minutes were we to meet.

Everything is now ready for you, except selecting the songs, but at all events you shall receive one more than our agreement. I can send you more bagatelles than I promised, as I have got ten others beside; if you write to me immediately, I will send you these, or as many as you wish for, along with the rest.

My health, indeed, is not entirely reestablished by the baths, yet on the whole I think I have improved. I had another annoyance here, owing to a person having engaged an unsuitable lodging for me, which is hard on me, as I cannot yet accustom myself to it, and my occupations are thus sadly deranged.

The case with regard to the Mass stands thus: I finished one long ago, and another is in progress. There is always a certain degree of gossip about people of our class, which has, no doubt, misled you. I don't yet know which you are to get. Besieged on all sides, I am almost forced to testify the reverse of the dictum that "the spirit cannot be weighed." I send you my best wishes, and trust that time will foster a beneficial and honorable connection between us.

BEETHOVEN.

311 - To the Archduke Rudolph.

I was extremely unwell both yesterday and the day before; unfortunately there was no one whom I could send to apprise Y.R.H. of the fact. As I felt better towards evening, I went into the town to make Schlemmer correct the Sonata.[1] He was not at home, so I requested him to come here to-day. I send the Sonata by him, and will come in to-day before four o'clock to wait on Y.R.H.

[K.]

*[**Note 1:** The C minor pianoforte Sonata, Op. 111?]*

312 - To Herr Peters.

Vienna, December 20, 1822.

I take advantage of a moment's leisure to-day to answer your letter. Not one of all the works that are your property is unfinished, but time is too precious to particularize all the details that prevent the copying and sending off the music to you. I recollect in a former letter having offered you some more bagatelles, but I by no means press you to take them. If you wish only to have the four, so be it; but in that case I must make a different selection. Herr ---- has not as yet got anything from me. Herr ---- begged me to make him a present of the songs for the "Journal de la Mode," which, in fact, I did not write for money; indeed, I find it quite impossible to act in every case according to so much per cent. It is painful for me to calculate in this manner oftener than is absolutely necessary. My position is far from being so brilliant as you think, &c., &c. It is not possible to listen to all these proposals at once, being far too numerous, but many cannot be refused. A commission is not always quite in accordance with the inclinations of an author. If my salary were not so far reduced as to be no salary at all,[1] I would write nothing but symphonies for a full orchestra, and church music, or at most quartets.

Of my minor works, you can still have Variations for two oboes and one English horn, on the theme from "Don Giovanni," "La ci darem la mano," and a Gratulation Minuet for a full orchestra. I should be glad, likewise, to have your opinion about the full edition of my works.

In the most desperate haste, your obedient

BEETHOVEN.

*[**Note 1:** It was reduced from 4000 gulden to 800.]*

313 - To F. Ries,--London

Vienna, December 20, 1822.

MY DEAR RIES,--

I have been so overburdened with work that I am only now able to reply to your letter of November 15. I accept with pleasure the proposal to write a new symphony for the Philharmonic Society. Although the prices given by the English cannot be compared with those paid by other nations, still I would gladly write even gratis for those whom I consider the first artists in Europe--were I not still, as ever, the poor Beethoven.

If I were only in London, what would I not write for the Philharmonic! For Beethoven, thank God! can write--if he can do nothing in the world besides! If Providence only vouchsafes to restore my health, which is at least improving, I shall then be able to respond to the many proposals from all parts of Europe, and even North America, and may thus perhaps be some day in clover.

314 - To Ignaz Ritter Von Seyfried.

1822.

My Dear and Worthy Brother in Apollo,--

I heartily thank you for the trouble you have taken in aiding my charitable work. [1] I rejoice that its success is universally admitted, and hope you will never fail to let me know when it is in my power to serve you by my poor talents. The worthy municipal corporation is, no doubt, thoroughly convinced of my good-will; in order to give fresh proofs of it, we ought to have a friendly interview as to the mode in which I can best serve the corporation. When such a master as yourself takes an interest in us, our pinions ought never to droop.

I am, with the warmest esteem,
Your friend,
BEETHOVEN.

*[**Note 1:** Seyfried, at a concert for the benefit of the Burgher Hospital, performed Beethoven's grand fugue Fest Ouverture (in C major, in Op. 124), 1822, in celebration of the opening of the new Josephstadt Theatre. The written parts were returned to him with the grateful thanks of the committee.]*

Third Part - Life's Troubles and Close - 1823 to 1827

315 - To Zelter.[1]

Vienna, Feb. 8, 1823.

MY BRAVE COLLEAGUE IN ART,--

I write, having a favor to ask of you, for we are now so distant from each other that we can no longer converse together, and, indeed, unhappily, we can seldom write either. I have written a grand mass, which might also be given as an oratorio (for the benefit of the poor, a good established custom here). I do not wish to publish it in the usual way, but to dispose of it to some of the leading courts alone. I ask fifty ducats for it. No copies are to be sold except those subscribed for, so that the mass will be, as it were, in manuscript; but there must be a fair number of subscribers, if any profit is to accrue to the author. I have made an application to the Prussian embassy here, to know if the King of Prussia would vouchsafe to take a copy, and I have also written to Prince Radziwill, to ask him to interest himself in the affair. I beg you likewise to do what you can for me. It is a work that might likewise be useful to the Academy of Singing, for there is scarcely any portion of it that could not be almost entirely executed by voices. The more these are increased and multiplied in combination with instruments, the more effective would be the result. It ought to be appropriate also as an oratorio, for such societies as those for the benefit of the poor require marks of this kind. Having been an invalid for some years past, and consequently my position anything but brilliant, I have had recourse to this scheme. I have written much; but as to profits, they are nearly nil! The more do I look upwards; but both for his own sake, and that of others, man is obliged to turn his eyes earthwards; for this, too, is part of the destiny of humanity. I embrace you, my dear fellow-artist, and am, with sincere esteem,

Your friend,
BEETHOVEN.

*[**Note 1:** Zelter was in Vienna in 1819.]*

316 - To F. Ries,--London.

... Manage this as soon as you can for your poor friend. I also expect my travelling route from you. Things have become quite too bad here, and I am fleeced worse than ever. If I do not go at all, lo! and behold a crimen laesae!... As it seems that you wish soon to have a dedication from me, I gladly comply with your request, much more so than with that of any great man; though, entre nous, the devil alone can tell how soon one may fall into their hands! The dedication to you will be written on the new symphony; and I hope I shall at length receive yours to me.

B. is to open the letter he took charge of for the King [George IV.], in which he will see what I have written to His Majesty on the subject of the "Battle of Vittoria." The tenor of the enclosed is the same; but not a word as to the mass.[1] Our amiable friend B. must try to get me at least a battle-axe or a turtle for it! The engraved copy of the score of "The Battle" must also be presented to the King. This letter will cost you a good deal [seventeen shillings]; but I beg you will deduct it from your remittance to me. How much I regret being so troublesome! May God prosper you!

Say all that is amiable to your wife till I come myself. Beware! you think me old; but I am a young veteran!

Yours, as ever,

B.

*[**Note 1:** On February 24, 1823, Beethoven wrote to the King of England that, so far back as 1813, he had sent him "Wellington's Victory," but never had received any communication on the subject; he, therefore, now sent an engraved copy of the work, which had been intended for him since 1815. He closed the letter by saying: "Convinced of the discrimination and kindness which your Majesty has always evinced in protecting and encouraging art and artists, the undersigned ventures to hope that your Majesty will graciously take the matter into consideration, and vouchsafe to comply with his respectful solicitation."]*

317 - To Schindler.

MY VERY BEST OPTIMUS OPTIME,--

Pray try to hunt out a philanthropist who will advance me some money on a bank-share, that I may not put the generosity of my friends too much to the test, nor myself be placed in difficulty by the delay of this money, for which I have to thank the fine plans and arrangements of my precious brother.

You must not let it appear that this money is really wanted.

318 - To Schindler.

DEAR SCHINDLER,--

Don't forget the bank-share. It is greatly needed; it would be very annoying to be brought into court; indeed, I would not be so for the whole world. My brother's conduct is quite worthy of him. The tailor is appointed to come today, still I hope to be able to get rid of him for the present by a few polite phrases.

319 - To Herr Kind.

DEAR KIND,--

I intend to call on you at latest on Wednesday afternoon at four o'clock, when I will settle everything.

Your obedient
BEETHOVEN.

320 - To Cherubini.[1]

March 15, 1823.

HIGHLY ESTEEMED SIR,--

I joyfully take advantage of this opportunity to address you. I have done so frequently in spirit, as I prize your theatrical works beyond others. The artistic world has only to lament that, in Germany at least, no new dramatic piece of yours has appeared. Highly as all your works are valued by true connoisseurs, still it is a great loss to art not to possess any fresh production of your great genius for the theatre.

True art is imperishable, and the true artist feels heartfelt pleasure in grand works of genius, and that is what enchants me when I hear a new composition of yours; in fact, I take greater interest in it than in my own; in short, I love and honor you. Were it not that my continued bad health prevents my going to see you in Paris, with what exceeding delight would I discuss questions of art with you! Do not think that this is merely intended to serve as an introduction to the favor I am about to ask of you. I hope and feel convinced that you do not for a moment suspect me of such base sentiments.

I recently completed a grand solemn mass, and have resolved to offer it to the various European courts, as it is not my intention to publish it at present. I have therefore solicited the King of France, through the French embassy here, to subscribe to this work, and I feel certain that his Majesty would, at your recommendation, agree to do so. Ma situation critique demande que je ne fixe pas seulement, comme ordinnaire, mes voeux au ciel; au contraire, il faut les fixer aussi ["aussi" in Beethoven's hand] en bas pour les nécessités de la vie. Whatever may be the fate of my request to you, I shall forever continue to love and esteem you, et vous resterez toujours celui de mes contemporains que je l'estime le plus. Si vous me voulez faire un extrême plaisir, c'était si vous m'écrivez quelques lignes, ce que me soulagera bien. L'art unit tout le monde, how much more, then, true artists, et peut-être vous me dignez aussi to include me in that number. Avec le plus haut estime,

Votre ami et serviteur,

BEETHOVEN.

*[**Note 1:** Cherubini declared that he never received this letter.]*

321 - To Schindler.[1]

DEAR SCHINDLER,--

I am not sure whether the other copy was corrected or not, so I send you this one instead. As to N. in S----, I beg you not to say a word; Bl. is already very uneasy on the subject. In haste, your friend,

BEETHOVEN.

*[**Note 1:** We cannot understand what induced Beethoven, who lived in the same house with Schindler, to write to him; but he often did so to persons with whom he could easily have spoken, partly in order to get rid of the matter while it was in his thoughts, and also because he was a great deal from home; that is, going backwards and forwards from one lodging to another, having often several at the same time.]*

322 - To Herr Peters,--Leipzig.

Vienna, March 20, 1823.

The other three marches are only to be sent off to-day, as I missed the post last week. Irregular as I have been on this occasion in our transactions, you would not think me so culpable if you were here, and aware of my position, a description of which would be too tedious both for you and me.

I have now an observation to make with regard to what I have sent off to you.

Several sets of wind instruments may combine in the performance of the Grand March, and if this cannot be done, and a regimental band is not strong enough for its present arrangement, any bandmaster can easily adapt it by omitting some of the parts.

You can, no doubt, find some one in Leipzig to show you how this can be managed with a smaller number, although I should regret if it were not to appear engraved exactly as it is written.

You must forgive the numerous corrections in the works I send; my old copyist no longer sees distinctly, and the younger one has yet to be trained, but at all events there are no errors left.

It is impossible for me to comply at once with your request for a stringed and a pianoforte quartet, but if you will write to me fixing the time you wish to have both works, I will do what I can to complete them. I must, however, apprise you that I cannot accept less than 50 ducats for a stringed quartet, and 70 for a pianoforte one, without incurring loss; indeed, I have repeatedly been offered more than 50 ducats for a violin quartet. I am, however, always unwilling to ask more than necessary, so I adhere to the sum of 50 ducats, which is, in fact, nowadays the usual price.

The other commission is indeed an uncommon one, and I, of course, accept it, only I must beg you to let me know soon when it is required; otherwise, willing as I am to give you the preference, I might find it almost impossible to do so. You know I wrote to you formerly that quartets were precisely what had risen most in value, which makes me feel positively ashamed when I have to ask a price for a really great work. Still, such is my position that it obliges me to secure every possible advantage. It is very different, however, with the work itself; when I never, thank God, think of profit, but solely of how I write it. It so happens that two others besides yourself wish to have a mass of mine, and I am quite disposed to write at least three. The first has long been finished, the second not yet so, and the third not even begun. But in reference to yourself, I must have a certainty, that I may in any event be secure.

More of this next time I write; do not remit the money, at any rate till you hear from me that the work is ready to be sent off.

I must now conclude. I hope your distress is, by this time, in some degree alleviated.

Your friend,
BEETHOVEN.

323 - To Zelter.

Vienna, March 25, 1823.

SIR,--

I avail myself of the present opportunity to send you my best wishes. The bearer of this asked me to recommend her to you; her name is Cornega; she has a fine mezzo soprano, and is a very artistic singer, and has, moreover, been favorably received in several operas.

I have also specially considered your proposals about your Academy for Singing. If the Mass is ever published, I will send you a copy free of all charge. There is no doubt that it might be almost entirely executed à la capella; in which case, however, the work would have to be arranged accordingly; perhaps you have patience to do this. Besides, there is already a movement in the work quite à la capella, and that style may be specially termed the true church style. Thanks for your wish to be of service to me, but never would I accept anything whatever from so highly esteemed an artist as yourself. I honor you,

and only wish I could have an opportunity to prove this by my actions.

I am, with high consideration,
Your friend and servant,
BEETHOVEN.

324 - To His Imperial Highness the Archduke Rudolph.

The Spring of 1823.

YOUR IMPERIAL HIGHNESS,--

It must still be some days before I can wait on you again, as I am in the greatest hurry to send off the works that I named to your R.H. yesterday, for if they are not punctually dispatched, I might lose all profit. Your R.H. can easily understand how much time is occupied in getting copies made, and looking through every part; indeed, it would not be easy to find a more troublesome task. Your R.H. will, I am sure, gladly dispense with my detailing all the toil caused by this kind of thing, but I am compelled to allude to it candidly, though only in so far as is absolutely necessary to prevent your R.H. being misled with regard to me, knowing, alas! only too well what efforts are made to prejudice your R.H. against me. But time will prove that I have been in all respects most faithful and attached to your R.H., and if my position were only as great as my zeal to serve your R.H., no happier man than myself would exist.

I am your R.H.'s faithful and obedient servant,
BEETHOVEN.

325 - To Schindler.

Imprimis.--Papageno, not a word of what I said about Prussia. No reliance is to be placed on it; Martin Luther's table-talk alone can be compared to it. I earnestly beg my brother also not to remove the padlock from his lips, and not to allow anything to transpire beyond the Selchwurst-Gasse.[1]

Finis.--Inquire of that arch-churl Diabelli when the French copy of the Sonata in C minor [Op. 111] is to be published. I stipulated to have five copies for myself, one of which is to be on fine paper, for the Cardinal [the Archduke Rudolph]. If he attempts any of his usual impertinence on this subject, I will sing him in person a bass aria in his warehouse which shall cause it and all the street (Graben) to ring![2]

*[**Note 1:** Schindler relates: "The royal decision (to subscribe for a copy of the mass) was brought to Beethoven by the Chancellor of the Embassy, Hofrath*

Wernhard. Whether Prince Hatzfeld [the Ambassador] made the following offer from his own impulse, or in consequence of a commission from Berlin, is not known. At all events, the Hofrath put this question in the name of the prince to the great composer, 'Whether he would be disposed to prefer a royal order to the fifty ducats' [the sum demanded for the mass]. Beethoven replied at once, 'The fifty ducats.' Scarcely had the Chancellor left the room when Beethoven, in considerable excitement, indulged in all kinds of sarcastic remarks on the manner in which many of his contemporaries hunted after orders and decorations, these being in his estimation generally gained at the cost of the sanctity of art."]

*[**Note 2:** Schindler relates that Diabelli had refused to let Beethoven again have the MS. of the Sonata, which he had repeatedly sent for when in the hands of the engraver, in order to correct and improve it. Diabelli therefore coolly submitted to all this abuse of the enraged composer, and wrote to him that he would note down the threatened bass aria, and publish it, but would give him the usual gratuity for it, and that Beethoven had better come to see him. On this Beethoven said no more. This Sonata is dedicated to the Archduke Rudolph, and is also published by Schlesinger.]*

326 - To F. Ries,--London.

Vienna, April 25, 1823.

DEAR RIES,--

The Cardinal's stay here of a month robbed me of a great deal of time, being obliged to give him daily lessons of two or three hours each; and after such lessons I was scarcely able next day to think, far less to write. My continued melancholy situation compels me, however, to write immediately what will bring me in sufficient money for present use. What a sad revelation is this! I am, besides, far from well, owing to my many troubles,--weak eyes among others.

But do not be uneasy, you shall shortly receive the Symphony; really and truly, my distressing condition is alone to blame for the delay. In the course of a few weeks you shall have thirty-three new variations on a theme [Valse, Op. 120] dedicated to your wife.

Bauer [First Secretary to the Austrian Embassy] has the score of the "Battle of Vittoria," which was dedicated to the then Prince Regent, and for which I have still to receive the costs of copying. I do beg you, my dear friend, to remit me as soon as possible anything you can get for it. With regard to your tender conjugal discussion, you will always find an opponent in me,--that is, not so much an opponent of yours as a partisan of your wife's. I remain, as ever, your friend,

BEETHOVEN.

327 - To Herr Lissner,--Petersburg.

Vienna, May 7, 1823.

SIR,--

Herr v. Schuppanzigh assured me, when he was here, that you were anxious to acquire some of my productions for your house. Perhaps the following works might suit your purpose, namely: six bagatelles for pianoforte, 20 gold ducats; thirty-five variations on a favorite theme for pianoforte, forming one entire work, 30 gold ducats; two grand airs with chorus, the poetry by Goethe and Matthisson, which can be sung either with instrumental or pianoforte accompaniment, 12 gold ducats.

I request an answer as soon as possible, for others also wish to have my works.

I am, sir, your obedient
LUDWIG VAN BEETHOVEN.

328 - To Schindler.

[1]
Hetzendorf, 1823.

SAMOTHRACIAN VAGABOND!--[2]

You must hunt out from Schlemmer [the copyist] what is still wanting in the "Kyrie;" show him the postscript, and so, satis, no more of such a wretch! Farewell! arrange everything; I am to bind up my eyes at night, and to spare them as much as possible; otherwise, says Smetana, I shall write little more music in the time to come.

*[**Note 1:** "We arrived at Hetzendorf on May 17" is written by Carl in Beethoven's note-book of 1823; and on this note is written, in the "scamp's" hand, Hetzendorf, 1823.]*

*[**Note 2:** "By the word 'Samothracian,' Beethoven alludes to the Samothracian Mysteries, partly grounded on music. Their mutual participation in the Beethoven Mysteries is intended to be thus indicated. Among the initiated were also Brunswick, Lichnowsky, and Zmeskall." [From a note of Schindler's on the subject.]]*

329 - To Schindler.

Hetzendorf, 1823 (?).

Pray, forward the packet to-day, and inquire this afternoon, if possible, about the housekeeper in the Glockengasse, No. 318, 3d Étage. She is a widow, understands cookery, and is willing to serve merely for board and lodging, to which, of course, I cannot consent, or only under certain conditions. My present one is too shameful. I cannot invite you here, but be assured of my gratitude.

330 - To Schindler.[1]

Hetzendorf, 1823.

I enclose the letter to Herr v. Obreskow [Chargé d'Affaires of the Russian Legation]; as soon as I receive the money, I will immediately send you 50 florins for your trouble. Not a word more than what is absolutely necessary!

I have advertised your house. You can mention, merely as a casual remark at the right moment, that France also remitted the money to you.

Never forget that such persons represent Majesty itself.

*[**Note 1:** Louis VIII. sent a gold medal for his subscription copy of the Mass on February 20, 1824.]*

331 - To Schindler.

I beg you will kindly write out the enclosed invitation neatly for me on the paper I send you, for Carl has too much to do. I wish to dispatch it early on Wednesday. I want to know where Grillparzer lives; perhaps I may pay him a visit myself.[1] You must have a little patience about the 50 florins; as yet it is impossible for me to send them, for which you are as much to blame as I am.

*[**Note 1:** It is well known that in the winter of 1822-23 Beethoven was engaged in the composition of an opera for the Royal Theatre; for which purpose Grillparzer had given him his Melusina.]*

332 - To Schindler.

I send K.'s [Kanne's] book [libretto]. Except the first act, which is rather insipid, it is written in such a masterly style that it does not by any means require a first-rate composer. I will not say that on this very account it would be the more suitable for me; still, if I can get rid of previous engagements, who knows what may or will happen! Please acknowledge the receipt of this.

333 - To Schindler.

I wish to know about Esterhazy, and also about the post. A letter-carrier from the Mauer [a place near Hetzendorf] was here; I only hope the message has been properly delivered. Nothing as yet from Dresden [see No. 330]. I mean to ask you to dine with me a few days hence, for I still suffer from my weak eyes; to-day, however, for the first time, they seem to improve, but I scarcely dare make any use of them as yet.

Your friend,
BEETHOVEN.

P.S. As for the Tokay,[1] it is better adapted for summer than for autumn, and also for some fiddler who could respond to its noble fire, and yet stand firm as a rock.

*[**Note 1:** A musical friend had sent the maestro six bottles of genuine Tokay, expressing his wish that it might tend to restore his strength. Schindler, he says, wrote to Beethoven at Hetzendorf, to tell him of this, and received the above answer, and the order through "Frau Schnaps" to do as he pleased with the wine. He sent one bottle of it to Hetzendorf, but Beethoven at that time had inflamed eyes.]*

334 - To Schindler.

I cannot at present accept these tempting invitations [from Sonntag and Unger]; so far as my weak eyes permit, I am very busy, and when it is fine, I go out. I will myself thank these two fair ladies for their amiability. No tidings from Dresden. I shall wait till the end of this month, and then apply to a lawyer in Dresden. I will write about Schoberlechner to-morrow.

335 - To Schindler.

June 18, 1823.

You ought to have perfectly well known that I would have nothing to do with the affair in question. With regard to my being "liberal," I think I have shown you that I am so on principle; indeed, I suspect you must have observed that I even have gone beyond these principles. Sapienti sat.[1]

*[**Note 1:** Franz Schoberlechner, pianist in Vienna, wrote to Beethoven on June 25, 1823, to ask him for letters of introduction to Leipzig, Dresden, Berlin, and Russia, etc. The maestro, however, wrote across the letter, "An active fellow requires no other recommendation than from one respectable family to another," and gave it back to Schindler, who showed it to Schoberlechner, and no doubt at his desire urged Beethoven to comply with his request. Beethoven, however, did not know Schoberlechner, and had no very high opinion of him, as he played chiefly bravura pieces, and, besides, on the bills of his concerts, he pompously paraded all his titles, decorations, and as member of various societies, which gave ample subject for many a sarcastic remark on the part of Beethoven.]*

336 - To the Archduke Rudolph.

Vienna, June 1, 1823.

I have been always ailing since Y.R.H. left this, and latterly afflicted by severe inflammation of the eyes, which has now in so far subsided that for the last eight days I have been able once more to use my sight, though very sparingly. Y.R.H. will perceive from the enclosed receipt of June 27, the dispatch of some music. As Y.R.H. seemed to take pleasure in the C minor Sonata,[1] I thought I did not take too much on myself by surprising Y.R.H. with the dedication. The Variations[2] have been written out for at least five or six weeks past, but the state of my eyes did not permit me to revise them thoroughly myself. My hope of being entirely restored proved vain. At last I made Schlemmer look them over, so, though they may not look very neat, still they are correct. The C minor Sonata was engraved in Paris in a very faulty manner, and being engraved here from that copy, I tried to make it as correct as possible. I intend shortly to send you a beautifully engraved copy of the Variations. With regard to the Mass[3] that Y.R.H. wished should be more generally known, my continued bad health for some years past, causing me to incur heavy debts, and compelling me to give up my intention of going to England, induced me to ponder on some mode of improving my condition. This Mass seemed well adapted to my purpose. I was advised to offer it to different courts. Painful as this was to me, I felt that I should have cause for self-reproach if I neglected doing so. I therefore applied to various courts to subscribe to the Mass, fixing the price at fifty ducats; the general opinion being that this was not too much, and if there were a good many subscribers, the scheme would not be unprofitable. Hitherto the subscription is indeed flattering to me, as their Majesties of France and Prussia have each taken a copy. I also received a letter from my friend Prince Nicolaus Gallizin a few days ago, from Petersburg, in which this most amiable Prince mentions that H.M. the Emperor of Russia had become a subscriber, and that I should soon hear further on the subject from the Imperial Russian Embassy. Notwithstanding all this (and though there are some other subscribers), I have not yet realized as much as the sum a publisher offered me for it; the only advantage being that the work remains mine. The costs of copying are also great, and further increased by three new pieces being added, which, as soon as they are completed, I will send to Y.R.H. Perhaps you would not think it too much trouble to apply to H.R.H. the Grand Duke of Tuscany to take a copy of this Mass. The application was indeed made some time ago to the Grand Duke of Tuscany through the agent here, V. Odelga, who faithfully assured me that the proposal would be graciously accepted. I place no great faith, however, in this, as some months have elapsed, and no notice has been again taken of the application. As the affair is now set agoing, it is but natural that I should do all I can to attain my desired object. The undertaking was from the first disagreeable to me, and still more so to mention it to Y.R.H., or to allude to it at all, but "necessity has no law." I only feel grateful to Him who dwells above the stars that I now begin once more to be able to use my eyes. I am at present writing a new symphony for England,[4] bespoken by the Philharmonic Society, and hope it will be quite finished fourteen days hence. I cannot strain my eyes as yet long at a time; I beg therefore Y.R.H.'s indulgence with regard to your Variations,[5] which appear to me very charming, but still require closer revision on my part. Y.R.H. has only to persevere, especially to accustom yourself to write down your ideas at once at the piano, quickly and briefly. For this purpose a small table ought to be placed close beside the piano. By this means not only is the imagination strengthened; but you learn instantly to hold fast the most fugitive ideas. It is equally necessary to be able to write without any piano; and sometimes a simple choral melody, to be carried out in simple or varied phrases, in counterpoint, or in a free manner, will certainly entail no headache on Y.R.H., but rather, in finding yourself thus right amid the centre of art, cause you very great pleasure. The faculty of representing precisely what we wish and feel comes by degrees; an essential desideratum for a noble-minded man. My eyes warn me to conclude. With every kind and good wish for Y.R.H., I remain, &c., &c.

[K.]

Postscript.

If Y.R.H. should confer the happiness of a letter on me, I beg you will address to me at Vienna, for I shall receive all my letters here safely forwarded by the post from there. If agreeable to Y.R.H., I would beg you to recommend the Mass to Prince Anton in Dresden,[6] so that the King of Saxony may subscribe to it, which he will, no doubt, do if Y.R.H. shows any interest in the matter. As soon as I know that you have actually done me this favor, I will forthwith apply to the General-Director there[7] of the Royal Theatre and of Music, whose office it is to arrange these things, and send him a request to procure a subscription from the King of Saxony, which I am reluctant to do without a recommendation from Y.R.H.

My opera, "Fidelio," was performed with much applause in Dresden at the festivities there in honor of the visit of the King of Bavaria, when their Majesties were all present. I received this intelligence from the above-named director-general, who asked me for the score through Weber, and afterwards sent me really a very handsome present in return. I hope Y.R.H. will excuse my intruding such a request on you, but Y.R.H. knows that I am not usually importunate. Should, however, the slightest obstacle arise to render my request disagreeable to you, I shall not be the less convinced of your generosity and kindness. Neither avarice, nor the love of speculation, which I have always avoided, prompted this scheme; but necessity compels me to use every effort to rescue my self from my present condition. Candor is best, for it will prevent my being too hardly judged. Owing to constant ill health, which has prevented my writing as usual, I have incurred a debt of 200 to 300 florins C.M.,[8] which can only be discharged by vigorous exertions on my part. If my subscription succeeds better than it has hitherto done, it will be an effectual help, and if my health improves, of which there is every hope, I shall be able once more to resume my compositions with fresh energy. In the mean time I trust Y.R.H. will not be offended by my candor. Had it not been the fear of being accused of not sufficiently bestirring myself, I would have persevered in my usual silence. As to the recommendation, I am at all events convinced that Y.R.H. is always glad to effect good results for others when possible, and that you are not likely to make any exception in my case.

*[**Note 1:** This Sonata, Op. 111, dedicated to the Archduke Rudolph, was composed in 1822, and published by Schlesinger in the beginning of 1823.]*

*[**Note 2:** These Variations are, no doubt, the 33 C major Variations for pianoforte, Op. 120, on a waltz of Diabelli's, dedicated to Madame Brentano, composed in 1823, and published in the June of the same year.]*

*[**Note 3:** The Grand Mass in D.]*

*[**Note 4:** The symphony which Beethoven declared he had completed in fourteen days was the 9th in D minor, composed in 1822 or 1823, first performed on the 7th May, and published in 1826.]*

*[**Note 5:** The Archduke's Variations alluded to by Beethoven are not published or now known.]*

*[**Note 6:** In a letter from the Archduke Rudolph of July 31, 1823, he says, "My brother-in-law, Prince Anton, has written to me that the King of Saxony is expecting your beautiful Mass."]*

*[**Note 7:** The director-general of the musical Court band and opera in Dresden (1823) was Von Könneritz.]*

*[**Note 8:** This debt of 200 to 300 florins had only been incurred by Beethoven in order not to sell out his shares in the Austrian Loan; he was in no need.]*

337 - To Schindler.

Hetzendorf, July 1, 1823.

I am myself writing to Wocher [cabinet courier to Prince Esterhazy? No. 333], and for more speed I send by Carl, who chances to be driving in, the application to Prince E. Be so good as to inquire the result; I doubt its being favorable, not expecting much kindly feeling on his part towards me, judging from former days.[1] I believe that female influence alone ensures success with him in such matters; at all events, I now know, by your obliging inquiries, how I can safely write to this Scholz. The bad weather, and more especially the bad atmosphere, prevented my paying her [Countess Schafgotsch] a visit about this affair.[2]

Your amicus,
BEETHOVEN.

P.S. Nothing yet from Dresden! Schlemmer [the copyist] has just been here asking again for money. I have now advanced him 70 Gulden. Speculations are for commercial men, and not for poor devils like myself. Hitherto the sole fruit of this unlucky speculation [a subscription for his Mass] are only more debts. You have, no doubt, seen that the "Gloria" is completed. If my eyes were only strong again, so that I could resume my writing, I should do well enough. [Written on the cover:] Are the Variations [Op. 120] sent off yet to London? N.B.--So far as I can remember, it was not mentioned in the application to Prince Ester-

hazy that the Mass was to be delivered in manuscript only. What mischief may ensue from this! I suspect that such was the intention of Herr Artaria in proposing to present the Mass gratis to the Prince, as it would give Artaria an opportunity for the third time to steal one of my works. Wocher's attention must be called to this.

Of course, there is nothing obligatory on Papageno in the matter.

*[**Note 1:** Beethoven wrote the Mass in C for him in the year 1807, which was by no means satisfactory to the prince when performed at Eisenstadt in the year following, and conducted by Beethoven himself.]*

*[**Note 2:** Scholz, music director at Warmbrunn in Silesia, had written a German text for the Mass in C. Beethoven also wished to have from him a German translation from the Latin words adapted to the music of the Grand Mass. Schindler says, that the words "prevented my visiting her" refer to Countess Schafgotsch, whom Beethoven wished to see on account of Scholz, who unhappily died in the ensuing year. His text, however, is given in the Cecilia, 23-54.]*

338 - To Pilat, Editor of the "Austrian Observer."

SIR,--

I shall feel highly honored if you will be so good as to mention in your esteemed journal my nomination as an honorary member of the Royal Swedish Musical Academy. Although neither vain nor ambitious, still I consider it advisable not wholly to pass over such an occurrence, as in practical life we must live and work for others, who may often eventually benefit by it. Forgive my intrusion, and let me know if I can in any way serve you in return, which it would give me much pleasure to do.

I am, sir, with high consideration,
Your obedient
BEETHOVEN.

339 - To Schindler.

Hetzendorf, July, 1823.

MOST WORTHY RAGAMUFFIN OF EPIRUS AND BRUNDUSIUM!--

Give this letter to the editor of the "Observer," but write the address on it first; ask him at the same time whether his daughter makes great progress on the piano, and if I can be of any use to her by sending her a copy of one of my compositions. I wrote that I was an "honorary member;" I don't know, however, whether this is correct; perhaps I ought to have said, "a corresponding member;" neither knowing nor caring much about such things. You had also better say something on the subject to Bernardum non sanctum (editor of the "Vienna Zeitschrift"). Make inquiries, too, from Bernard about that knave Ruprecht; tell him of this queer business, and find out from him how he can punish the villain. Ask both these philosophical newspaper scribes whether this may be considered an honorable or dishonorable nomination.

340 - To Schindler.

Master flash in the pan, and wide of the mark! full of reasons, yet devoid of reason!--Everything was ready yesterday for Gläser (the copyist). As for you, I shall expect you in Hetzendorf to dinner at half-past two o'clock. If you come later, dinner shall be kept for you.

341 - To Schindler.

Hetzendorf, July 2, 1823.

WORTHY HERR V. SCHINDLER,--

The incessant insolence of my landlord from the hour I entered his house up to the present moment compels me to apply for aid to the police; so I beg you will do so for me at once. As to the double winter windows, the housekeeper was desired to see about them, and especially to state if they were not necessary after such a violent storm, in case of the rain having penetrated into the room; but her report was that the rain had not come in, and, moreover, that it could not possibly do so. In accordance with her statement, I locked the door to prevent this rude man entering my room during my absence (which he had threatened). Say also further what his conduct to you was, and that he put up a placard of the lodgings being to let, without giving me notice, which, besides, he has no right to do till St. James's Day. He is equally unfair in refusing to give up the receipt from St. George's Day till St. James's, as the enclosure shows; I am charged, too, for lighting, of which I know nothing. This detestable lodging,[1] without any open stove, and the principal flue truly abominable, has cost me (for extra outlay, exclusive of the rent) 259 florins, in order merely to keep me alive while I was there during the winter. It was a deliberate fraud, as I never was allowed to see the rooms on the first floor, but only those on the second, that I might not become aware of their many disagreeable drawbacks. I cannot understand how a flue so destructive to health can be tolerated by the Government. You remember the appearance of the walls of your room owing to smoke, and the large sum it cost even to lessen in any degree this discomfort, although to do away with it wholly was impossible. My chief anxiety at present is that he may be ordered to take down his placard, and to give me a receipt for the house-rent I have paid; but nothing will induce me to pay for the abominable lighting, without which it cost me enough actually to preserve my life in such a lodging. My eyes do not yet suffer me to encounter the town atmosphere, or I would myself apply in person to the police.

Your attached
BEETHOVEN.

*[**Note 1:** The Pfarrgasse, in the Laimgrube, where Schindler lived with him.]*

342 - To Schindler.

I must have an attested copy of all the writings; I send you 45 kreutzers. How could you possibly accept such a proposal from our churlish landlord when accompanied by a threat? Where was your good sense? Where it always is.

To-morrow early I shall send for the Variations, copy and originals. It is not certain whether the Pr. comes or not; so be so good as to stay at home till eight o'clock. You can come to dinner either to-day or to-morrow; but you must settle which you mean to do, as it is not easy for me to provide provisions. Not later than half-past two o'clock. The housekeeper will tell you about a lodging in the Landstrasse. It is high time, truly! As soon as you hear of anything to be had on the Bastei or the Landstrasse, you must at once give me notice. We must find out what room the landlord uses on account of the well.--Vale!

343 - To Schindler.[1]

Hetzendorf, 1823.

SAMOTHRACIAN VAGABOND!--

You were dispatched yesterday to the South Pole, whereas we went off to the North Pole, a slight difference now equalized by Captain Parry. There were, however, no mashed potatoes there.

Bach [his lawyer], to whom I beg my best regards, is requested to say what the lodging in Baden is to cost; we must also try to arrange that Carl should come to me once every fortnight there (but cheaply; good heavens! poverty and economy!). I intrust this matter to you, as you have your friends and admirers among the drivers and liverymen. If you get this in time, you had better go to Bach to-day, so that I may receive his answer to-morrow forenoon. It is almost too late now.

You might also take that rascal of a copyist by surprise; I don't expect much good from him. He has now had the Variations for eight days.

Your ["friend" stroked out] amicus,
BEETHOVEN.

*[**Note 1:** He no doubt alludes to Captain Parry, the celebrated traveller, who wrote an article in the A.M. Zeitung on the music of the Esquimaux.]*

344 - To Schindler.[1]

June, 1823.

SAMOTHRACIAN!-- Don't trouble yourself to come here till you receive a Hati Scherif. I must say you do not deserve the golden cord. My fast-sailing frigate, the worthy and well-born Frau Schnaps, will call every three or four days to inquire after your health.

Farewell! Bring no one whatever with you: farewell!

*[**Note 1:** Schindler says in his Biography: "These Variations [Op. 120] were completed in June, 1823, and delivered to the publisher, Diabelli, without the usual amount of time bestowed on giving them the finishing touches; and now he set to work at once at the ninth Symphony, some jottings of which were already written down. Forthwith all the gay humor that had made him more sociable, and in every respect more accessible, at once disappeared. All visits were declined," &c.]*

345 - To the Archduke Rudolph.

Hetzendorf, July 15, 1823.

I trust that you are in the best possible health. As for my eyes, they are improving, though slowly, and in six or seven days at most I hope to have the good fortune to wait on Y.R.H. If I were not obliged to use spectacles, I should get better sooner. It is a most distressing occurrence, and has thrown me back in everything. What soothes my feelings, however, is Y.R.H. being fully aware that I am always to be of service to you. I have another favor to ask of Y.R.H., which I hope you will graciously accede. Will Y.R.H. be so kind as to grant me a testimonial to the following effect: "That I wrote the Grand Mass expressly for Y.R.H.; that it has been for some time in your possession; and that you have been pleased to permit me to circulate it." This ought to have been the case, and being no untruth, I hope I may claim this favor. Such a testimonial will be of great service to me; for how could I have believed that my slight talents would have exposed me to so much envy, persecution, and calumny. It has always been my intention to ask Y.R.H.'s permission to circulate the Mass, but the pressure of circumstances, and above all my inexperience in worldly matters, as well as my feeble health, has caused this confusion.

If the Mass is engraved hereafter, I hope to dedicate it to Y.R.H. when published,[1] and not till then will the limited list of royal subscribers appear. I shall ever consider Y.R.H. as my most illustrious patron, and make this known to the world whenever it is in my power. In conclusion, I entreat you again not to refuse my request about the testimonial. It will only cost Y.R.H. a few lines, and ensure the best results for me.

I will bring the Variations[2] of Y.R.H. with me. They require little alteration, and cannot fail to become a very pretty pleasing work for all lovers of music. I must indeed appear a most importunate suitor. I beg you will kindly send me the testimonial as soon as possible, for I require it.

[K.]

*[**Note 1:** The Grand Mass (Op. 123) was published in 1827.]*

*[**Note 2:** The Variations composed by the Archduke Rudolph, mentioned in the letters 345 and 351, are not the same as the published ones, and are unknown.]*

346 - To F. Ries.

Hetzendorf, July 16, 1823.

MY DEAR RIES,--

I received your letter with much pleasure the day before yesterday. The Variations have, no doubt, arrived by this time. I could not write the dedication to your wife, not knowing her name; so I beg you will write it yourself on the part of your wife's friend and your own; let it be a surprise to her, for the fair sex like that.--Entre nous, surprise is always the greatest charm of the beautiful! As for the Allegri di Bravura, I must make allowance for yours. To tell you the truth, I am no great friend to that kind of thing, as it is apt to entail too much mere mechanism; at least, such is the case with those I know. I have not yet looked at yours, but I shall ask ---- about them. I recommend you to be cautious in your intercourse with him. Could I not be of use to you in many ways here? These printers, or rather misprinters, as they ought to be called to deserve their names, pirate your works, and give you nothing in return; this, surely, might be differently managed. I mean to send you some choruses shortly, even if obliged to compose some new ones, for this is my favorite style.

Thanks for the proceeds of the bagatelles, with which I am quite satisfied. Give nothing to the King of England. Pray accept anything you can get for the Variations. I shall be perfectly contented. I only must stipulate to take no other reward for the dedication to your wife than the kiss which I am to receive in London.

You name guineas, whereas I only get pounds sterling, and I hear there is a difference between these. Do not be angry with un pauvre musicien autrichien, who is still at a very low ebb. I am now writing a new violin quartet. Might not this be offered to the musical or unmusical London Jews?--en vrai Juif.

I am, with cordial regard,
Your old friend,
BEETHOVEN.

347 - To Herr Geheimrath von Könneritz,--Dresden,Director of the Royal Orchestra and Theatre in Saxony.

[1]
Hetzendorf, July 17, 1823.

SIR,--

I have too long deferred sending you a signed receipt and thanks, but I feel sure you will pardon the delay from my great pressure of business, owing to my health having improved, and God knows how long this may continue. The description given by my dear friend Maria Weber[2] of your generous and noble disposition encourages me to apply to you on another subject, namely, about a Grand Mass which I am now issuing in manuscript. Though I have met with a previous refusal on this matter [337], still, as my esteemed Cardinal, H.R. Highness the Archduke Rudolph, has written to H.R.H. Prince Anton, requesting him to recommend the Mass to his Majesty the King of Saxony, I think this fresh application might at all events be made, as I should consider it a great honor to number among my distinguished subscribers (such as the King of Prussia, the Emperor of Russia, the King of France, &c.) so great a connoisseur in music as the King of Saxony.

I leave it to you, sir, to decide from this statement how and when you can best effect my purpose. I am unable to send you to-day the application for a subscription to my Mass to H.M. the King of Saxony, but I will do so by the next post. In any event I feel assured that you will not think I am one of those who compose for the sake of paltry gain; but how often do events occur which constrain a man to act contrary to his inclinations and his principles? My Cardinal is a benevolent Prince, but means are wanting! I hope to receive your forgiveness for my apparent importunity. If my poor abilities can in any way be employed in your service, what extreme pleasure it would give me.

I am, sir, with esteem,
Your expectant
BEETHOVEN.

*[**Note 1:** The director-general of the Dresden theatre at that time was Von Könneritz, who sent Beethoven forty ducats (requesting a receipt) for his opera of Fidelio, performed with great applause April 29, 1823, and conducted by C.M. von Weber. Madame Schröder-Devrient made her début in the character of Leonore.]*

*[**Note 2:** In Weber's Biography it is stated (Vol. II. p. 465) that Beethoven and Weber exchanged several letters about the performance of Fidelio, and in fact Weber did receive letters from Beethoven on February 16, April 10, and June 9. Unhappily, no part of this correspondence has yet been discovered, except a fragment of the sketch of a letter written by Weber of January 28, 1823, which sufficiently*

proves that Beethoven was right in calling him his friend. It is as follows:--"This mighty work, teeming with German grandeur and depth of feeling, having been given under my direction at Prague, had enabled me to acquire the most enthusiastic and instructive knowledge of its inner essence, by means of which I hope to produce it before the public here with full effect, provided as I am with all possible accessories for the purpose. Each performance will be a festival to me, permitting me to pay that homage to your mighty spirit which dwells in the inmost recesses of my heart, where love and admiration strive for the mastery." On October 5 of this year, Weber visited Beethoven in Baden, with Haslinger and Benedict.]

348 - To Herr V. Könneritz,--Dresden.

Vienna, July 25, 1823.

SIR,--

Forgive my importunity in sending to your care the enclosed letter from me to his R.H. Prince Anton of Saxony; it contains an application to his Majesty the King of Saxony to subscribe to a mass of mine. I recently mentioned to you that the Cardinal Archduke Rudolph had written to his M. the King of Saxony about this Mass; I entreat you to use all your influence in this matter, and I leave it entirely to your own judgment and knowledge of local matters to act as you think best. Although I do not doubt that the recommendation of my Cardinal will have considerable weight, still the decision of his Majesty cannot fail to be much influenced by the advice of the Administrator of objects connected with the fine arts. Hitherto, in spite of apparent brilliant success, I have scarcely realized as much as a publisher would have given me for the work, the expenses of copying being so very great. It was the idea of my friends to circulate this Mass, for, thank God! I am a mere novice in all speculations. In the mean time, there is not a single employé of our Government who has not been, like myself, a loser. Had it not been for my continued bad health for many years past, a foreign country would at least have enabled me to live free from all cares except those for art. Judge me kindly, and not harshly; I live only for my art, and my sole wish is to fulfil my duties as a man; but this, alas! cannot always be accomplished without the influence of the subterranean powers. While commending my cause to you, I also venture to hope that your love of art, and above all your philanthropy, will induce you to be so good as to write me a few lines, informing me of the result as soon as you are acquainted with it.

I am, sir, with high consideration,
Your obedient
BEETHOVEN.

349 - To Schindler.

August, 1823.

YOU SAMOTHRACIAN VILLAIN!--Make haste and come, for the weather is just right. Better early than late--presto, prestissimo! We are to drive from here.[1]

*[**Note 1:** Beethoven had apartments in a summer residence of Baron Pronay's on his beautiful property at Hetzendorf. Suddenly, however, the maestro, deeply immersed in the Ninth Symphony, was no longer satisfied with this abode, because "the Baron would persist in making him profound bows every time that he met him." So, with the help of Schindler and Frau Schnaps, he removed to Baden in August, 1823.]*

350 - To His Nephew.

Baden, August 16, 1823.

MY DEAR BOY,--

I did not wish to say anything to you till I found my health improving here, which, however, is scarcely even yet the case. I came here with a cold and catarrh, which were very trying to me, my constitution being naturally rheumatic, which will, I fear, soon cut the thread of my life, or, still worse, gradually wear it away. The miserable state of my digestive organs, too, can only be restored by medicines and diet, and for this I have to thank my faithful servants! You will learn how constantly I am in the open air when I tell you that to-day for the first time I properly (or improperly, though it was involuntary) resumed my suit to my Muse. I must work, but do not wish it to be known. Nothing can be more tempting (to me at least) than the enjoyment of beautiful Nature at these baths, but nous sommes trop pauvres, et il faut écrire ou de n'avoir pas de quoi. Get on, and make every preparation for your examination, and be unassuming, so that you may prove yourself higher and better than people expect. Send your linen here at once; your gray trousers must still be wearable, at all events at home; for, my dear son, you are indeed very dear to me! My address is, "At the coppersmith's," &c. Write instantly to say that you have got this letter. I will send a few lines to that contemptible creature, Schindler, though I am most unwilling to have anything to do with such a wretch. If we could write as quickly as we think and feel, I could say a great deal not a little remarkable; but for to-day I can only add that I wish a certain Carl may prove worthy of all my love and unwearied care, and learn fully to appreciate it.

Though not certainly exacting, as you know, still there are many ways in which we can show those who are better and nobler than ourselves that we acknowledge their superiority.

I embrace you from my heart.
Your faithful and true
FATHER.

351 - To the Archduke Rudolph.

August, 1823.

I am really very ill, and not suffering from my eyes alone. I intend to drag myself to-morrow to Baden, to look out for a lodging, and to go there altogether in the course of a few days. The air in town has a very bad effect on my whole organization, and has really injured my health, having gone twice to town to consult my physicians. It will be easier for me to repair to Y.R.H. in Baden. I am quite inconsolable, both on account of Y.R.H. and myself, that my usefulness is thus limited. I have marked some things in the Variations, but I can explain these better verbally.

[K.]

352 - To the Archduke Rudolph.

Baden, August 22, 1823.

Your gracious letter led me to believe that Y.R.H. intended to return to Baden, where I arrived on the 13th, very ill; but I am now better. I had recently another inflammatory cold, having just recovered from one. My digestion, too, was miserable, and my eyes very bad; in short, my whole system seemed impaired. I was obliged to make the effort to come here, without even being able to see Y.R.H. Thank God, my eyes are so much better that I can again venture to make tolerable use of them by daylight. My other maladies, too, are improving, and I cannot expect more in so short a period. How I wish that Y.R.H. were only here, when in a few days we could entirely make up for lost time. Perhaps I may still be so fortunate as to see Y.R.H. here, and be able to show my zeal to serve Y.R.H. How deeply does this cause me to lament my unhappy state of health. Much as I wish for its entire restoration, still I greatly fear that this will never be the case, and on this account I hope for Y.R.H.'s indulgence. As I can now at length prove how gladly I place myself at Y.R.H.'s disposal, my most anxious desire is that you would be pleased to make use of me.

[K.]

353 - To the Archduke Rudolph.

1823.

I have just been enjoying a short walk and composing a Canon, "Grossen Dank, ÷ ÷ ÷," when, on returning home, with the intention of writing it out for

Y.R.H., I find a petitioner who is under the delusion that his request will be better received if made through me. What can I do? A good action cannot be too soon performed, and even a whim must be sometimes humored. The bearer of this is Kapellmeister Drechsler, of the Josephstadt and Baden Theatre; he wishes to obtain the situation of second Court organist. He has a good knowledge of thorough bass, and is also a good organist, besides being favorably known as a composer,--all qualities that recommend him for this situation. He rightly thinks that the best recommendation to secure him the appointment is that of Y.R.H., who, being yourself so great a connoisseur and performer, know better than any one how to appreciate true merit; and assuredly H.I. Majesty would prefer such testimony to every other. I therefore add my entreaties, though with some hesitation, to those of Herr D., relying on the indulgence and kindness of Y.R.H., and in the hope that the illustrious patron and protector of all that is good will do what lies in his power to be of use on this occasion.

My Canon shall be sent to-morrow,[1] together with the confession of my sins, intentional and unintentional, for which I beg your gracious absolution. My eyes, alas! prevent me from saying to-day as I could wish my hopes and desires that all good may attend you.

P.S. I ought also to mention that Herr Drechsler is the unsalaried professor of thorough bass at St. Anna's, and has been so for the last ten years.

[K.]

*[**Note 1:** The Canon, Grossen Dank, ÷ ÷ ÷, is not to be found in either Breitkopf & Härtel's or Thayer's catalogue, nor anywhere else.]*

354 - To F. Ries.

Baden, September 5, 1823.

MY DEAR FRIEND,--

You advise me to engage some one to look after my affairs; now I did so as to the Variations; that is, my brother and Schindler took charge of them, but how?

The Variations were not to have appeared here till after being published in London; but everything went wrong. The dedication to Brentano [Antonie v. Brentano, née Edlen von Birkenstock] was to be confined to Germany, I being under great obligations to her, and having nothing else to spare at the moment; indeed, Diabelli, the publisher, alone got it from me. But everything went through Schindler's hands. No man on earth was ever more contemptible,--an arch villain; but I soon sent him packing! I will dedicate some other work to your wife in the place of this one. You, no doubt, received my last letter [No. 346]. I think thirty ducats would be enough for one of the Allegri di Bravura, but I should like to publish them here at the same time, which might easily be arranged. Why should I give up so much profit to these rogues here? It will not be published here till I am told that it has arrived in London; moreover, you may yourself fix the price, as you best know London customs.

The copyist to-day at last finished the score of the Symphony; so Kirchhoffer and I are only waiting for a favorable opportunity to send it off. I am still here, being very ill when I arrived, and my health still continues in a most precarious condition, and, good heavens! instead of amusing myself like others at these baths, my necessities compel me to write every day. I am also obliged to drink the mineral waters besides bathing. The copy will shortly be sent off; I am only waiting till I hear of an opportunity from Kirchhoffer, for it is too bulky to forward by post.

My last letter must have given you an insight into everything. I will send you some choruses; let me have any commissions for oratorios as soon as you can, that I may fix the time at once. I am sorry about the Variations on account of ----, as I wrote them more for London than here. This is not my fault. Answer me very soon, both as to particulars and time. Kind regards to your family.

355 - To F. Ries,--London.

Baden, September 5, 1823.

MY DEAR KIND RIES,--

I have still no tidings of the Symphony, but you may depend on its soon being in London. Were I not so poor as to be obliged to live by my pen, I would accept nothing from the Philharmonic Society; but as it is, I must wait till the money for the Symphony is made payable here; though as a proof of my interest and confidence in that Society, I have already sent off the new Overture, and I leave it to them to settle the payment as they please.

My brother, who keeps his carriage, wished also to profit by me; so without asking my permission, he offered this Overture to Boosey, a London publisher. Pray, tell him that my brother was mistaken with regard to the Overture. I see now that he bought it from me in order to practise usury with it. O Frater!!

I have never yet received the Symphony you dedicated to me. If I did not regard this dedication as a kind of challenge to which I am bound to respond, I would ere this have dedicated some work to you. I always, however, wished first to see yours, and how joyfully would I then testify my gratitude to you in one way or another.

I am, indeed deeply your debtor for your kind services and many proofs of attachment. Should my health improve by my intended course of baths, I hope to kiss your wife in London in 1824.

Yours, ever,
BEETHOVEN.

356 - To the Archduke Rudolph.

1823.

I have just heard that Y.R.H. is expected here to-morrow. If I am still unable to follow the impulse of my heart, I hope you will ascribe it to the state of my eyes. I am better, but for some days to come I dare not breathe the town air, so prejudicial to my eyes. I only wish that the next time Y.R.H. returns from Baden, you would be so good as to let me know, and also name the hour at which I am to present myself, and once more have the good fortune to see my gracious master. But as it is probable Y.R.H. will not long remain here, it is the more incumbent on us to take advantage of the short time at our disposal to carry out our artistic discussions and practice. I will myself bring "Grossen Dank, ÷ ÷ ÷," as it must be sent to Baden. Herr Drechsler thanked me to-day for the liberty I had taken in recommending him to Y.R.H., who received him so graciously that I beg to express my warmest gratitude for your kindness. I trust that Y.R.H. will continue firm, for it is said that Abbé Stadler is endeavoring to procure the situation in question for some one else. It would also be very beneficial to Drechsler if Y.R.H. would vouchsafe to speak to Count Dietrichstein[1] on the subject. I once more request the favor of being told the date of your return from Baden, when I will instantly hasten into town to wait on the best master I have in this world. Y.R.H.'s health seems to be good; Heaven be praised that it is so, for the sake of so many who wish it, and among this number I may certainly be included.

[K.]

*[**Note 1:** Count Moritz Dietrichstein was in 1823 Court director of the royal band.]*

357 - To the Archduke Rudolph.

I was very much affected on receiving your gracious letter yesterday. To flourish under the shade of a stately verdant fruit-tree is refreshing to any one capable of elevated thought and feeling, and thus it is with me under the aegis of Y.R.H. My physician assured me yesterday that my malady was disappearing, but I am still obliged to swallow a whole bottle of some mixture every day, which weakens me exceedingly, and compels me, as Y.R.H. will see from the enclosed instructions of the physician, to take a great deal of exercise. I have every hope, however, that soon, even if not entirely recovered, I shall be able to be a great deal with Y.R.H. during your stay here. This hope will tend to recruit my health sooner than usual. May Heaven bestow its blessings on me through Y.R.H., and may the Lord ever guard and watch over you! Nothing can be more sublime than to draw nearer to the Godhead than other men, and to diffuse here on earth these godlike rays among mortals. Deeply impressed by the gracious consideration of Y.R.H. towards me, I hope very soon to be able to wait on you.

[K.]

358 - To Schindler.

Baden, September, 1823.

SIGNORE PAPAGENO,--

That your scandalous reports may no longer distress the poor Dresdener, I must tell you that the money reached me to-day, accompanied by every possible mark of respect to myself.

Though I should have been happy to offer you a substantial acknowledgment for the [illegible, effaced by Schindler] you have shown me, I cannot yet accomplish to the full extent what I have so much at heart. I hope to be more fortunate some weeks hence. [See No. 329.]

Per il Signore Nobile, Papageno Schindler.

359 - To Schindler.

1823.

The occurrence that took place yesterday, which you will see in the police reports, is only too likely to attract the notice of the established police to this affair. The testimony of a person whose name is not given entirely coincides with yours. In such a case private individuals cannot act; the authorities alone are empowered to do so.[1]

Yours,
BEETHOVEN.

*[**Note 1:** Schindler says, "Brother Johann, the apothecary, was ill in the summer of 1823, and during that time his disreputable wife visited her lover, an officer, in the barracks, and was often seen walking with him in the most frequented places, besides receiving him in her own house. Her husband, though confined to bed, could see her adorning herself to go in search of amusement with her admirer. Beethoven, who was informed of this scandal from various quarters, appealed vigorously to his brother, in the hope of persuading him to separate from his ill-conducted wife, but failed in his attempt, owing to the indolence of this ill-regulated man." It was Schindler, too, who prevented Beethoven making any further application to the police. The following note probably refers to this. In his note-book of November, 1823, is a Canon written by Beethoven on his brother Johann and his family, on these words, "Fettlümerl Bankert haben triumphirt," no doubt an allusion to the disgraceful incident we have mentioned. Brother Johann's wife had a very lovely daughter before she married him.]*

360 - To Schindler.

WISEACRE! I kiss the hem of your garment!

361 - To Herr Grillparzer, Court Composer.

ESTEEMED SIR,--

The directors wish to know your terms with regard to "Melusina." [See No. 331.] In so far she has asserted herself, which is certainly better than being obliged to importune others on such matters. My household has been in great disorder for some time past, otherwise I should have called on you, and requested you to visit me in return.[1] Pray, write your conditions at once, either to the directors or to myself, in which case I will undertake to deliver them. I have been so busy that I could not call on you, nor can I do so now, but hope to see you before long. My number is 323.

In the afternoons you will find me in the coffee-house opposite the "Goldene Birne." If you do come, I beg that you may be alone. That obtrusive appendage, Schindler, has long been most obnoxious to me, as you must have perceived when at Hetzendorf,[2] otium est vitium. I embrace and esteem you from my heart.

Yours,
BEETHOVEN.

*[**Note 1:** In the note-book of 1823 is written, in Beethoven's hand:*

8th or 9th November, bad humor.
Another bad day.
Another bad day.

And underneath, in Schindler's hand:
Devil take such a life!]

*[**Note 2:** The Elegante Zeitung of 1858, No. 73, relates the following anecdote about this visit:--"During the composition of the Opera many conferences took place between the two artistic colleagues, when the new work was zealously discussed on both sides. On one occasion the poet drove out to visit the composer in the country. Beethoven's writing-desk was placed somewhat like a sentry-box opposite a cupboard for provisions, the contents of which compelled the housekeeper to be perpetually coming and going, attracting thereby many an admonitory look askance in the midst of his conversation from the deaf maestro. At last the clock struck the dinner-hour. Beethoven went down to his cellar, and soon after returned carrying four bottles of wine, two of which he placed beside the poet, while the other two were allotted to the composer himself and a third guest. After dinner Beethoven slipped out of the room, and held a short parley with the coachman hired for the occasion, who was still waiting at the door. When the time arrived for re-*

turning to town, Beethoven proposed driving part of the way with his guests, and did not get out of the carriage till close to the Burgthor. Scarcely was he gone when the companions he had just quitted found some papers lying on the seat he had vacated, which proved to be six gulden, the amount of the carriage-hire. They instantly stopped the carriage, and shouted to their friend (who was making off as quick as he could) that he had forgotten some money; but Beethoven did not stand still till he was at a safe distance, when he waved his hat, rejoicing with the glee of a child at the success of his trick. There was no possibility of refusing his naïf generosity, and they had sufficient delicacy of feeling not to poison his enjoyment by any untimely remonstrances."]

362 - To Probst, Music Publisher,--Leipzig.

Vienna, March 10, 1824.

... These are all I can at present give you for publication. I must, alas! now speak of myself, and say that this, the greatest work I have ever written, is well worth 1000 florins C.M. It is a new grand symphony, with a finale and voice parts introduced, solo and choruses, the words being those of Schiller's immortal "Ode to Joy," in the style of my pianoforte Choral Fantasia, only of much greater breadth. The price is 600 florins C.M. One condition is, indeed, attached to this Symphony, that it is not to appear till next year, July, 1825; but to compensate for this long delay, I will give you a pianoforte arrangement of the work gratis, and in more important engagements you shall always find me ready to oblige you.

363 - To Schindler.

1824.

Frau S. [Schnaps] will provide what is required, so come to dinner to-day at two o'clock. I have good news to tell you,[1] but this is quite entre nous, for the braineater [his brother Johann] must know nothing about it.

*[**Note 1:** This no doubt refers to a letter from Prince Gallizin, March 11, 1824:--"I beg you will be so good as to let me know when I may expect the Quartet, which I await with the utmost impatience. If you require money, I request you will draw on Messrs. Stieglitz & Co., in St. Petersburg, for the sum you wish to have, and it will be paid to your order."]*

364 - To Herr V. Rzehatschek.

1824.

MY WORTHY HERR V. RZEHATSCHEK,--

Schuppanzigh assures me that you intend to be so kind as to lend me the instruments required for my concert; [1] thus encouraged, I venture to ask you to do so, and hope not to meet with a refusal when thus earnestly soliciting you to comply with my request.

Your obedient servant,
BEETHOVEN.

*[**Note 1:** It seems highly probable that this concert is the celebrated one in the spring of 1824, when the Ninth Symphony and a portion of the Grand Mass were performed.]*

365 - To the High Chamberlain Prince Trautmannsdorf. [1]

I am deeply indebted to your Highness for your invariable politeness, which I prize probably the more from Y.H. being by no means devoid of sympathy for my art. I hope one day to have the opportunity of proving my esteem for your H.

*[**Note 1:** Enclosed in a note to Schindler, who was to apply for the great Redoutensaal for the concert on April 8, 1824.]*

366 - To Count Moritz Lichnowsky. [1]

Insincerity I despise; visit me no more; my concert is not to take place.

BEETHOVEN.

*[**Note 1:** The originals of these three well-known notes were found by Schindler on the piano, where Beethoven usually left things of the kind, which he intended his amanuensis to take charge of. Lichnowsky, Schuppanzigh, and Schindler had all met at Beethoven's, as if by chance, in order to discuss with him some difficulties which stood in the way of the concert. The suspicious maestro saw only collusion and treachery in this, and wrote these notes, which Schindler did not allow to be sent.]*

367 - To Herr Schuppanzigh.

Come no more to see me. I give no concert.
BEETHOVEN.

368 - To Herr Schindler.

Do not come to me till I summon you. No concert.
BEETHOVEN.

369 - To Herr V. Sartorius, Royal Censor.

SIR,--

As I hear that obstacles are likely to arise on the part of the royal censorship to a portion of sacred music being given at an evening concert in the Theatre "an der Wien," I must inform you that I have been particularly requested to give these pieces, that the copies for this purpose have already caused serious expense, and the intervening time is too short to produce other new works. Besides, only three sacred compositions are to be given, and these under the title of hymns. I do earnestly entreat you, sir, to interest yourself in this matter, as there are always so many difficulties to contend with on similar occasions. Should this permission not be granted, I do assure you that it will be impossible to give a concert at all, and the whole outlay expended on the copying be thrown away. I hope you have not quite forgotten me.

I am, sir, with high consideration, yours,
BEETHOVEN.

370 - To Schindler.

1824.

If you have any information to give me, pray write it down; but seal the note, for which purpose you will find wax and a seal on my table. Let me know where Duport[1] lives, when he is usually to be met with, and whether I could see him alone, or if it is probable that people will be there, and who?

I feel far from well. Portez-vous bien. I am still hesitating whether to speak to Duport or to write to him, which I cannot do without bitterness.

Do not wait dinner for me; I hope you will enjoy it. I do not intend to come, being ill from our bad fare of yesterday. A flask of wine is ready for you.

*[**Note 1:** Schindler says that on April 24, 1824, he applied to Duport, at that time administrator of the Kärnthnerthor Theatre, in Beethoven's name, to sanction his giving a grand concert there, allowing him to have the use of the house for the sum of 400 florins C.M. Further, that the conducting of the concert should be intrusted to Umlauf and Schuppanzigh, and the solos to Mesdames Unger and Sonntag, and to the bass singer Preisinger.]*

371 - To Schindler.

[1]

I beg you will come to see me to-morrow, as I have a tale to tell you as sour as vinegar. Duport said yesterday that he had written to me, though I have not yet got his letter, but he expressed his satisfaction, which is best of all.

The chief feat however is not yet performed, that which is to be acted in front of the Proscenium!

[In Beethoven's writing:] Yours, from C# below to high F,

BEETHOVEN.

*[**Note 1:** Written by his nephew.]*

372 - To Schindler.

After six weeks of discussion, here, there, and everywhere, I am fairly boiled, stewed, and roasted. What will be the result of this much-talked-of concert if the prices are not raised? What shall I get in return for all my outlay, as the copying alone costs so much?

373 - To Schindler.

At twelve o'clock to-day "in die Birne" [an inn on the Landstrasse]--thirsty and hungry--then to the coffee-house, back again here, and straight to Penzing, or I shall lose the lodging.

374 - To Schindler.

When you write to me, write exactly as I do to you, without any formal address or signature--vita brevis, ars longa. No necessity for details; only the needful!

375 - To Herr Steiner & Co.

Baden, May 27, 1824.

P.N.G. [PATERNOSTERGÄSSEL],--

Have the goodness to give me a proof of your great complaisance, by using your hand-rostrum (ruler) (not Rostrum Victoriatum) to rule 202 lines of music for me, somewhat in the style I now send, and also on equally fine paper, which you must include in your account. Send it, if possible, to-morrow evening by Carl, for I require it.

Perhaps plenary indulgence may then be granted.

376 - Pour M. De Haslinger, Général Musicien Et Général-Lieutenant.

MY DEAR FRIEND,--

You would really do me great injustice were you to suppose that negligence prevented my sending you the tickets; I assure you that it was my intention to do so, but I forgot it like many other things. I hope that some other opportunity may occur to enable me to prove my sentiments with regard to you. I am, I assure you, entirely innocent of all that Duport has done, in the same way that it was he who thought fit to represent the Terzet [Op. 116] as new, not I. You know too well my love of truth; but it is better to be silent now on the subject, as it is not every one who is aware of the true state of the case, and I, though innocent, might incur blame. I do not at all care for the other proposals Duport makes, as by this concert I have lost both time and money. In haste, your friend,

BEETHOVEN.

377 - To Steiner & Co.

MY KIND FRIEND,--

Be so good as to read the enclosed, and kindly forward it at once to the authorities.

Your servant and amicus,

BEETHOVEN.

378 - To Herr Tobias Peter Philip Haslinger.

The horn part and the score are shortly to follow. We are immensely indebted to you. Observe the laws. Sing often my Canon in silence,--per resurrectionem, &c. Farewell!

Your friend,

BEETHOVEN.

379 - To Haslinger.

Have the goodness to send me my shoes and my sword. You can have the loan of the "Eglantine" for six days, for which, however, you must give an acknowledgment. Farewell!

Yours,

BEETHOVEN.

380 - To Haslinger.

Baden, June 12.

MY GOOD FRIEND,--

Something worth having has been put in your way; so make the most of it. You will no doubt come off with a handsome fee, and all expenses paid. As for the March with Chorus [in the "Ruins of Athens," Op. 114], you have yet to send me the sheets for final revision, also the Overture in E flat ["To King Stephen," Op. 117]; the Terzet [Op. 116]; the Elegy [Op. 118]; the Cantata

["Meeresstille und glückliche Fahrt," Op. 112]; and the Opera. Out with them all! or I shall be on very little ceremony, your right having already expired. My liberality alone confers on you a larger sum than you do on me. I want the score of the Cantata for a few days, as I wish to write a kind of recitative for it; mine is so torn that I cannot put it together, so I must have it written out from the parts. Has the Leipzig musical paper yet retracted its lies about the medal I got from the late King of France?

I no longer receive the paper, which is a shabby proceeding. If the editor does not rectify the statement, I shall cause him and his consumptive chief to be harpooned in the northern waters among the whales.

Even this barbarous Baden is becoming enlightened, and now instead of gutten Brunn, people write guten Brun. But tell me what are they about in Paternoster Street?

I am, with all esteem for yourself, but with none for the barbarian Paternoster-Gässel,

Your devoted, incomparativo,

B----N.

Paternoster-Gässel primus will no doubt, like Mephistopheles, emit fiery flames from his jaws.

381 - To M. Diabelli.

SIR,--

Pray forgive my asking you to send me the score of my Mass,[1] being in urgent need of it; but I repeat that no public use is to be made of it until I can let you know how and when. It will be at first performed under my direction, with the addition of several new pieces composed expressly for it, which I will with pleasure send to you afterwards. There are certain conventionalities which must be observed, especially as I am so dependent on foreign connections, for Austria does not furnish me with the means of existence, and gives me nothing but vexation. I will soon appoint a day for you to visit Carl.

I remain, sir, with the highest esteem, yours,

BEETHOVEN.

*[**Note 1:** This letter seems to be addressed to Diabelli, who in the summer of 1824 begged the loan of the Mass in D for a few days, but neglected to return it.]*

382 - To Probst,--Leipzig.

Vienna, July 3, 1824

SIR,--

Overwhelmed with work and concerts, it is only now in my power to inform you that the works you wished to have are finished and transcribed, and can be delivered at any time to Herr Glöggl [music publisher in Vienna]. I therefore request you will transmit the 100 Viennese ducats to Herr Glöggl, and let me know when you have done so. I must conclude for to-day, and defer the pleasure of writing further till another opportunity. I am, with esteem, yours obediently,

BEETHOVEN. [1]

*[**Note 1:** Probst answered the letter as follows:--*

"August 18, 1824.

"The many gossiping reports about the differences between you and a publisher here in a similar transaction are the cause, I frankly own, of my wishing first to see your manuscript. The piracy in engraving, so universal in Austria, often prevents the German publisher paying the price for a work which it merits; and even at this moment in Vienna, with regard to your compositions [Schindler mentions three songs with pianoforte accompaniment, six bagatelles, and a grand overture], I can see that the birds of prey are on the watch to rob me of them under the shelter of the law."

On one of these letters Beethoven writes in pencil, "Do not listen to gossip; I have no time at this moment to enter on the subject, but I have all the proofs in my own hands; more of this hereafter."]

383 - To T. Haslinger. [1]

MY VERY WORTHY FRIEND,--

Have the goodness to send me the Rochlitz article on the Beethoven works, and we will return it to you forthwith by the flying, driving, riding, or migrating post.

Yours,

BEETHOVEN.

*[**Note 1:** The Rochlitz'sche article is probably the report in the A.M. Zeitung of the works performed at the grand concert of May 7.]*

384 - To Herr Schott,--Mayence.

1824.

The Overture [1] that you got from my brother was recently performed here, and I received many eulogiums on the occasion.

What is all this compared to the grandest of all masters of harmony above! above! above! Rightfully the Most High! While here below all is a mere mockery--Dwarfs--and the Most High!!

You shall receive the Quartet with the other works. You are open and candid, qualities which I never before found in publishers, and this pleases me. I say so in writing, but who knows whether it may not soon be in person? I wish you would transmit the sum due for the Quartet to P., as at this moment

I require a great deal of money, for I derive everything from foreign sources, and sometimes a delay occurs--caused by myself.

*[**Note 1:** The Overture to which he alludes is no doubt Op. 124, in C major, Zur Weihe des Hauses, published by Schott. It was performed in the great concert of May 23 of this year (1824), which in the estimation of a Beethoven, already absorbed in new great works, might well be termed "recently performed." Schott himself says the letter is written between July 3 and September 17, 1824.]*

385 - To the Archduke Rudolph.

Baden, August 23, 1824.

YOUR ROYAL HIGHNESS,--

I live--how?--the life of a snail. The unfavorable weather constantly throws me back, and at these baths it is impossible to command one's natural strength. A few days ago, Nägeli, a musical author and poet of considerable repute, wrote to me from Zurich; he is about to publish 200 poems, and among these some are suitable for musical composition. He urged me much to apply to Y.R.H. to request that you would be graciously pleased to subscribe to this collection. The price is very moderate, 20 groschen, or 1 florin 80 kreutzers. Were Y.R.H. to subscribe for six copies, it would immediately be noised abroad, although I am well aware that my illustrious master does not care for anything of the kind; it will suffice for the present if Y.R.H. will condescend to inform me of your will on the subject. The money can be paid when the copies arrive, probably a couple of months hence. I have conveyed Herr Nägeli's request, and now I must ask another favor, on his account, from myself. Everything cannot be measured by line and plummet; but Wieland says: "A little book may be well worth a few groschen." Will Y.R.H. therefore honor these poems by permitting your august name to be prefixed to them, as a token of your sympathy for the benefit of this man? the work is not likely to be quite devoid of value. Being convinced of Y.R.H.'s interest in all that is noble and beautiful, I hope I shall not fail in my intercession for Nägeli, and I beg that Y.R.H. will give me a written permission to inform Nägeli that you will be one of his subscribers.

I remain, with all dutiful fidelity and devotion, your R. Highness's obedient servant,

BEETHOVEN.

386 - To His Nephew.

Baden, August 29, 1824.

MY DEAR YOUNG SCAMP,--

How active our mahogany Holz [wood] is! My plans are decided. We will give the present quartet to Artaria, and the last to Peters. You see I have learned something; I now perceive why I first explored the path; it was for your sake, that you might find it smooth. My digestion is terribly out of order, and no physician! I wish to have some ready-made pens, so send some in a letter. Don't write to Peters on Saturday; we had better wait a little, to show him our indifference on the subject.

Since yesterday I have only taken some soup, and a couple of eggs, and drank nothing but water; my tongue is discolored; and without medicine and tonics, whatever my farcical doctor may say, my digestion will never improve.

The third quartet [in C sharp minor, Op. 131] also contains six movements, and will certainly be finished in ten or twelve days at most. Continue to love me, my dear boy; if I ever cause you pain, it is not from a wish to grieve you, but for your eventual benefit. I now conclude. I embrace you cordially. All I wish is that you should be loving, industrious, and upright. Write to me, my dear son. I regret all the trouble I give you, but it will not go on long. Holz seems inclined to become our friend. I expect a letter soon from [illegible].

Your faithful
FATHER.

387 - Rough Draft of a Letter to Peters.

1824.

I wrote to you that a quartet ["and a grand one too" is effaced] is ready for you; as soon, therefore, as you let me know that you will accept it for the 360 florins C.M., or 80 ducats, I will at once forward it to you. My works are now paid at a higher rate than ever; besides, you have only yourself to blame in this affair. Your own letters show what you formerly desired to have, and the works I sent you were what they ought to have been (the numerous pirated editions prove the truth of this); but the Quartet will convince you that, so far from wishing to take my revenge, I now give you what could not possibly be better, were it intended even for my best friend.

I beg that you will make no delay, so that I may receive your answer by the next post; otherwise I must forthwith return you the 360 florins C.M. I shall, at all events, be rather in a scrape, for there is a person who wishes to have not only this but another newly finished work of mine, though he does not care to take only one. It is solely because you have waited so long (though you are yourself to blame for this) that I separate the Quartet from the following one, now also completed. (Do you think that the latter ought to be also offered here? but, of course, cunningly and warily: comme marchand coquin!) You need have no misgivings that I am sending you something merely to fulfil my promise; no, I assure you on my honor as an artist that you may place me on a level with the lowest of men, if you do not find that it is one of my very best works.

388 - To Hans Georg Nägeli,--Zurich.

Baden, September 9, 1824.

MY MUCH-VALUED FRIEND,--

The Cardinal Archduke is in Vienna, and owing to my health, I am here. I only yesterday received from him a gracious written consent to subscribe to your poems, on account of the services you have rendered to the progress of music. He takes six copies of your work. I will shortly send you the proper address. An anonymous friend is also on the list of subscribers. I mean myself, for as you do me the honor to become my panegyrist, I will on no account allow my name to appear. How gladly would I have subscribed for more copies, but my means are too straitened to do so. The father of an adopted son, (the child of my deceased brother,) I must for his sake think and act for the future as well as for the present. I recollect that you previously wrote to me about a subscription; but at that time I was in very bad health, and continued an invalid for more than three years, but now I am better. Send also the complete collection of your lectures direct to the Archduke Rudolph, and, if possible, dedicate them to him; you are certain at all events to receive a present, not a very large one probably, but still better than nothing; put some complimentary expressions in the preface, for he understands music, and it is his chief delight and occupation. I do really regret, knowing his talents, that I cannot devote myself to him as much as formerly.

I have made various applications to procure you subscribers, and shall let you know as soon as I receive the answers. I wish you would also send me your lectures, and likewise Sebastian Bach's five-part Mass, when I will at once remit you the money for both. Pray, do not imagine that I am at all guided by self-interest; I am free from all petty vanity; in godlike Art alone dwells the impulse which gives me strength to sacrifice the best part of my life to the celestial Muse. From childhood my greatest pleasure and felicity consisted in working for others; you may therefore conclude how sincere is my delight in being in any degree of use to you, and in showing you how highly I appreciate all your merits. As one of the votaries of Apollo, I embrace you.

Yours cordially,
BEETHOVEN.

Write to me soon about the Archduke, that I may introduce the subject to his notice; you need take no steps towards seeking permission for the dedication. It will and ought to be a surprise to him.

389 - To His Nephew.

Baden, evening, September 14, 1824.

MY DEAR SON,--,

Whether it rains heavily to-morrow or not, stifling dust or pouring rain would be equally prejudicial to me. It does grieve me to know that you are so long with this demon; but, pray, strive to keep out of her way. You must give her a letter, written in my name, to the manager of the hospital, in which you must state that she did not come on the 1st, partly because she was unwell, and also from various people having come here to meet me, Basta cosi!

I send you 40 florins for the singing-master [corépétiteur]. Get a written receipt from him: how many mistakes are thus avoided! and this should be done by every one who pays money for another. Did not Holz bring Rampel's receipt [the copyist] unasked, and do not others act in the same way? Take the white waistcoat for yourself, and have the other made for me. You can bring the metronome with you; nothing can be done with it. Bring also your linen sheets and two coverlets, and some lead-pencils and patterns; be sure you get the former at the Brandstatt. And now farewell, my dear son; come to my arms as early as you can,--perhaps to-morrow. *[The paper is here torn away.]*

As ever, your faithful
FATHER.

P.S. All that could be done was to send you by the old woman's char à banc, which, however, including everything, costs 8 florins 36 kreutzers.

Do not forget anything, and be careful of your health.

390 - To Herr Nägeli.

Vienna, September 16, 1824.

MY ESTEEMED FRIEND,--

I gladly comply with your wish that I should arrange the vocal parts of my last Grand Mass for the organ, or piano, for the use of the different choral societies. This I am willing to do, chiefly because these choral associations, by their private and still more by their church festivals, make an unusually profound impression on the multitude, and my chief object in the composition of this Grand Mass was to awaken, and deeply to impress, religious feelings both on singers and hearers. As, however, a copy of this kind and its repeated revision must cause a considerable outlay, I cannot, I fear, ask less than 50 ducats for it, and leave it to you to make inquiries on the subject, so that I may devote my time exclusively to it.

I am, with high consideration,
Your obedient
BEETHOVEN.

391 - To Schott,--Mayence.

Baden, near Vienna, September 17, 1824.

The Quartet [Op. 127, in E flat major] you shall also certainly receive by the middle of October. Overburdened by work, and suffering from bad health, I really have some claim on the indulgence of others. I am here entirely owing to my health, or rather to the want of it, although I already feel better. Apollo and the Muses do not yet intend me to become the prey of the bony Scytheman, as I have yet much to do for you, and much to bequeath which my spirit dictates, and calls on me to complete, before I depart hence for the Elysian fields; for I feel as if I had written scarcely more than a few notes of music.

I wish your efforts all possible success in the service of art; it is that and science alone which point the way, and lead us to hope for a higher life. I will write again soon. In haste, your obedient

BEETHOVEN.

392 - To Hauschka.

Baden, September 23, 1824.

MY DEAR AND VALUED FRIEND,--

As soon as I arrive in town, I will write Bernard's Oratorio [see No. 257], and I beg you will also transmit him payment for it. We can discuss when we meet in town what we further require and think necessary, and in the mean-time, I appoint you High and Puissant Intendant of all singing and humming societies, Imperial Violoncello-General, Inspector of the Imperial Chasse, as well as Deacon of my gracious master, without house or home, and without a prebendary (like myself). I wish you all these, most faithful servant of my illustrious master, as well as everything else in the world, from which you may select what you like best.[1] That there may be no mistake, I hereby declare that it is our intention to set to music the Bernard Oratorio, the "Sieg des Kreuzes" and speedily to complete the same. Witness this our sign and seal,

LUDWIG VAN BEETHOVEN.

1st P.S. Take care that the venison is not devoured by rats or mice--you understand? Strive for better choice and variety.

Yours, as a Christian and in Apollo,

B.

2d P.S. As for the little flag on the white tower, we hope soon to see it waving again!

*[**Note 1:** An allusion to Hauschka's subserviency to all persons in high Court offices.]*

393 - To Herr Nägeli,--Zurich.

Vienna, November 17, 1824.

MY MUCH-VALUED FRIEND,--

Deeply absorbed in work, and not sufficiently protected against this late season of the year, I have again been ill; so believe me it was impossible for me to write to you sooner. With regard to your subscription, I have only succeeded in getting one subscriber for two copies, Herr v. Bihler, tutor in the family of His Imperial Highness the Archduke Carl; he tried to get the Archduke also, but failed. I have exerted myself with every one, but, unluckily, people are here actually deluged with things of the same kind. This is all that I can write to you in my hurry. I urged the matter, too, on Haslinger, but in vain; we are really poor here in Austria, and the continued pressure of the war leaves but little for art and science. I will see that the subscriptions are paid, but let me know distinctly where the money is to be sent to. I embrace you in spirit. Always rely on the high esteem of your true friend,
BEETHOVEN.

394 - To the Archduke Rudolph.

November 18, 1824.

YOUR ROYAL HIGHNESS,--

On my return from Baden, illness prevented my waiting on Y.R.H. according to my wish, being prohibited going out; thus yesterday was the first time I dared to venture again into the open air. When your gracious letter arrived, I was confined to bed, and under the influence of sudorifics, my illness having been caused by a chill; so it was impossible for me to rise. I feel sure that Y.R.H is well aware that I never would neglect the respect so properly your due. I shall have the pleasure of waiting on you to-morrow forenoon. Moreover, there will be no lack of opportunity here to awaken the interest Y.R.H. takes in music, which cannot fail to prove so beneficial to art,--ever my refuge, thank God!

I remain Y.R.H.'s obedient servant,
BEETHOVEN.

395 - To Schott,--Mayence.

Vienna, November 18, 1824.

I regret being obliged to tell you that some little time must yet elapse before I can send off the works. There was not in reality much to revise in the copies; but as I did not pass the summer here, I am obliged to make up for this now, by giving two lessons a day to H.R.H. the Archduke Rudolph. This exhausts me so much that it almost entirely unfits me for all else. Moreover, I cannot live on my income, and my pen is my sole resource; but no consideration is shown either for my health or my precious time. I do hope that this may not long continue, when I will at once complete the slight revision required. Some days ago I received a proposal which concerns you also; its purport being that a foreign music publisher was disposed, &c., &c., to form a connection with you, in order to guard against piracy. I at once declined the offer, having had sufficiently painful experience on these matters. (Perhaps this was only a pretext to spy into my affairs!)

396 - To Carl Holz.

I send you my greetings, and also wish to tell you that I am not going out to-day. I should be glad to see you, perhaps this evening after your office hours.

In haste, your friend,
BEETHOVEN.
I am by no means well.

397 - To Carl Holz.

MY WORTHY HOLZ--BE NO LONGER HOLZ [WOOD]!

The well-beloved government wishes to see me to-day at ten o'clock. I beg you will go in my place; but first call on me, which you can arrange entirely according to your own convenience. I have already written a letter to the powers that be, which you can take with you. I much regret being forced to be again so troublesome to you, but my going is out of the question, and the affair must be brought to a close,
Yours,
BEETHOVEN.

398 - To Schott,--Mayence.

Vienna, December 17 [Beethoven's birthday], 1824.

I write to say that a week must yet elapse before the works can be dispatched to you. The Archduke only left this yesterday, and much precious time was I obliged to spend with him. I am beloved and highly esteemed by him, but--I cannot live on that, and the call from every quarter to remember "that he who has a lamp ought to pour oil into it" finds no response here.

As the score ought to be correctly engraved, I must look it over repeatedly myself, for I have no clever copyist at present. Pray, do not think ill of me! Never was I guilty of anything base!

399.

March, 1825.

MY GOOD FRIENDS,--

Each is herewith appointed to his own post, and formally taken into our service, pledging his honor to do his best to distinguish himself, and each to vie with the other in zeal.

Every individual cooperating in this performance must subscribe his name to this paper.[1]

Schuppanzigh, (Manu propria.)

Weiss.

Linke, (M.P.)

Confounded violoncello of the great masters.

Holz, (M.P.)

The last, but only as to his signature.

*[**Note 1:** In reference to the rehearsals of the first production of the E flat major Quartet, Op. 127, in March, 1825.]*

400 - To Schindler.

The Spring of 1825.

I have waited till half-past one o'clock, but as the caput confusum has not come, I know nothing of what is likely to happen. Carl must be off to the University in the Prater; so I am obliged to go, that Carl, who must leave this early, may have his dinner first. I am to be found in the "Wilde Mann" [an inn in the Prater].

To Herr Schindler, Moravian numskull.[1]

*[**Note 1:** Schindler was a Moravian.]*

401 - To Linke, Violoncellist.[1]

DEAR LINKE,--

Having heard Herr v. Bocklet very highly spoken of, I think it would be advisable to ask him kindly to play in the trio at your concert. I do not know him myself, or I would have applied to him on your behalf. Always rely on me when it is in my power to serve you.

Yours truly,

BEETHOVEN.

*[**Note 1:** Bocklet, a pianist in Vienna, tells me that he rehearsed the Trio with Holz and Linke in 1825 or 1826 at Beethoven's.]*

402. -To * * *[1]

SIR,--

Through the stupidity of my housekeeper your mother was recently sent away from my house, without my having been informed of her visit. I highly disapprove of such incivility, especially as the lady was not even shown into my apartments. The rudeness and coarseness of the persons whom I am so unfortunate as to have in my service are well known to every one; I therefore request your forgiveness.

Your obedient servant,

L. V. BEETHOVEN.

*[**Note 1:** In the New Vienna Musik Zeitung the occasion of this note is thus related:--"In 1825, a well-known artist and dilettante in the composition of music published a book of waltzes, each of these being composed by the most popular and celebrated musicians of the day; as no one declined giving a musical contribution to the editor, the profits being intended to enable him to go to Carlsbad for the benefit of the waters there. The work met with unusual support and sympathy. It then occurred to the editor to apply for a contribution to the great Ludwig van Beethoven, with whom he had been acquainted in former days through his father and grandfather. The great musician at once, in the most gracious and amiable manner, promised to comply with the request, and sent him not only a waltz, but (the only one who did so) also a trio, desiring the editor to send in the course of a month for these works, which would by that time be completed. As the editor was in the mean time taken ill, he was not able to call for the work himself, and was thus obliged to give up this interesting visit. He therefore requested his mother to apply for the waltz, &c., and to express his thanks; but the housekeeper, to whom she gave her name, refused to admit her, saying she could not do so, 'for her master was in such a crazy mood.' As at this very moment Beethoven chanced to put his head in at the door, she hurried the lady into a dark room, saying, 'Hide yourself, as it is quite impossible that anyone can speak to him to-day,' getting out of the way herself as fast as she could. A couple of days afterwards Beethoven sent the waltz, &c., to the house of the musical editor in question, with the above letter."]*

403 - To F. Ries.

Vienna, April 9, 1825.

MY DEAR GOOD RIES,--

I write only what is most pressing! So far as I can remember in the score of the Symphony [the 9th] that I sent you, in the first hautboy, 242d bar, there stands  F E D instead of  F E E. I have carefully revised all the instrumental parts, but those of the brass instruments only partially, though I believe they are tolerably correct. I would already have sent you my score [for performance at the Aix musical festival], but I have still a concert in prospect, if indeed my health admits of it, and this MS. is the only score I possess. I must now soon go to the country, as this is the only season when I profit by it.

You will shortly receive the second copy of the "Opferlied;" mark it at once as corrected by myself, that it may not be used along with the one you already possess. It is a fine specimen of the wretched copyists I have had since Schlemmer's death. It is scarcely possible to rely on a single note. As you have now got all the parts of the finale of the Symphony copied out, I have likewise sent you the score of the choral parts. You can easily score these before the chorus commences, and when the vocal parts begin, it could be contrived, with a little management, to affix the instrumental parts just above the scored vocal parts. It was impossible for me to write all these out at once, and if we had hurried such a copyist, you would have got nothing but mistakes.

I send you an Overture in C, 6/8 time, not yet published; you shall have the engraved parts by the next post. A Kyrie and Gloria, two of the principal movements (of the solemn Mass in D major), and an Italian vocal duet, are also on their way to you. You will likewise receive a grand march with chorus, well adapted for a musical performance on a great scale, but I think you will find what I have already sent quite sufficient.

Farewell! You are now in the regions of the Rhine [Ries at that time lived at Godesberg, near Bonn], which will ever be so dear to me! I wish you and your wife every good that life can bestow! My kindest and best regards to your father, from your friend,

BEETHOVEN.

404 - To Herr Jenger,--Vienna.[1]

1824.

MY ESTEEMED FRIEND,--

It will give me much pleasure to send you some day soon the score of Matthisson's "Opferlied." The whole of it, published and unpublished, is quite at your service. Would that my circumstances permitted me to place at once at your disposal the greater works I have written, before they have been heard. I am, alas! fettered on this point; but it is possible that such an opportunity may hereafter occur, when I shall not fail to take advantage of it.

The enclosed letter is for Hofrath v. Kiesewetter. I beg you will be so good as to deliver it, especially as it concerns yourself quite as much as the Herr Hofrath.

I am, with high esteem, your devoted friend,

BEETHOVEN.

*[**Note 1:** This note is addressed to Jenger in Vienna, a chancery official and a musical amateur, connoisseur, factotum, and distinguished pianist. The date is not known. The Opferlied he refers to, is undoubtedly the 2d arrangement, Op. 121-b, which according to the Leipzig A.M. Zeitung was performed as Beethoven's "most recent poetical and musical work," at the concert in the Royal Redoutensaal, April 4, 1824.]*

405 - To Schott.

I have much pleasure in herewith contributing to the "Cecilia" [1] and its readers some Canons written by me, as a supplement to a humorous and romantic biography of Herr Tobias Haslinger residing here, which is shortly to appear in three parts.

In the first part, Tobias appears as the assistant of the celebrated and solid Kapellmeister Fux, holding the ladder for his Gradus ad Parnassum. Being, however, mischievously inclined, he contrives, by shaking and moving the ladder, to cause many who had already climbed up a long way, suddenly to fall down, and break their necks.

He now takes leave of this earthly clod and comes to light again in the second part in the time of Albrechtsberger. The already existing Fux, nota cambiata, is now dealt with in conjunction with Albrechtsberger. The alternating subjects of the Canon are most fully illustrated. The art of creating musical skeletons is carried to the utmost limit, &c.

Tobias begins once more to spin his web as a caterpillar, and comes forth again in the third part, making his third appearance in the world. His half-fledged wings bear him quickly to the Paternostergässel, of which he becomes the Kapellmeister. Having emerged from the school of the nota cambiata, he retains only the cambiata and becomes a member of several learned societies, &c. But here are the Canons.

On a certain person of the name of Schwencke. [2]

On a certain person of the name of Hoffmann.

LUDWIG VAN BEETHOVEN.

*[**Note 1:** A periodical published for the musical world, and edited by a society of savants, art-critics, and artists; Mayence, B. Schott & Sons. The publishers applied to Beethoven, in the name of the editors, for a contribution to the Cecilia.]*

*[**Note 2:** It appears that Kapellmeister Schwencke in Hamburg, in many complimentary and flowery phrases, had requested Beethoven to send him his autograph. Perhaps Beethoven, to whom the sound of certain names appeared comical, alludes here to this Hamburg Kapellmeister Schwencke.]*

406 - To Ludwig Rellstab.

May 3, 1825.

As I was just starting for the country yesterday, I was obliged to make some preparations myself; so unluckily your visit to me was in vain. Forgive me in consideration of my very delicate health. As perhaps I may not see you again, I wish you every possible prosperity. Think of me when writing your poems.

Your friend,
BEETHOVEN.

Convey my affectionate regards and esteem to Zelter,--that faithful prop of true art.

Though convalescent, I still feel very weak. Kindly accept the following token of remembrance from

Your friend,
BEETHOVEN.

407 - To * * *

Vienna.
SIR,--

Being on the point of going into the country, and only very recently recovered from an attack of internal inflammation, I can merely write you a few words. In the passage in the "Opferlied," 2d strophe, where it runs thus:--

I wish it to be written thus:--

408 - To His Brother Johann.

Baden, May 6, 1825.

The bell and bell-pulls, &c., &c., are on no account whatever to be left in my former lodging. No proposal was ever made to these people to take any of my things. Indisposition prevented my sending for it, and the locksmith had not come during my stay to take down the bell; otherwise it might have been at once removed and sent to me in town, as they have no right whatever to retain it. Be this as it may, I am quite determined not to leave the bell there, for I require one here, and therefore intend to use the one in question for my purpose, as a similar one would cost me twice as much as in Vienna, bell-pulls being the most expensive things locksmiths have. If necessary, apply at once to the police. The window in my room is precisely in the same state as when I took possession, but I am willing to pay for it, and also for the one in the kitchen,--2 florins 12 kreutzers for the two. The key I will not pay for, as I found none; on the contrary, the door was fastened or nailed up when I came, and remained in the same condition till I left; there never was a key, so of course neither I myself, nor those who preceded me, could make use of one. Perhaps it is intended to make a collection, in which case I am willing to put my hand in my pocket.

LUDWIG VAN BEETHOVEN.

409 - To Herr Von Schlemmer.[1]

SIR,--

It strikes me as very remarkable that Carl cannot be persuaded to go into good society, where he might amuse himself in a creditable manner. This almost leads me to suspect that he possibly finds recreations, both in the evening and at night, in less respectable company. I entreat you to be on your guard as to this, and on no pretext whatever to allow him to leave the house at night, unless you receive a written request from me to that effect, by Carl. He once paid a visit, with my sanction, to Herr Hofrath Breuning. I strongly recommend this matter to your attention; it is far from being indifferent, either to you or to me; so I would once more urge you to practise the greatest vigilance.

I am, sir,
Your obedient
BEETHOVEN.

*[**Note 1:** In 1825, his nephew lived with Schlemmer in the Alleengasse, close to the Karlskirche.]*

410 - To His Nephew.

Frau Schlemmer is to receive, or has already received, her money by our housekeeper. Some letters must be written to-morrow. Let me know what time would suit you best? Your

UNCLE.

I left my pocket-handkerchief with you.

411.[1]

My Dear Son,--

I have this moment got your letter. I still feel very weak and solitary, and only read the horrid letter I enclose! I send you 25 florins to buy the books at once, and you can spend the surplus when you require to do so. Pray bring me back Reisser's note.[2] On Saturday, the 14th of May, I will send a carriage into town to fetch you here; the charge is as yet very reasonable. The old woman is to inquire what hour will suit you best; you can set off at any time before six in the evening, so that you need neglect nothing. Perhaps I may come myself, and then your shirts might be purchased; in which case it would be as well if you were to be at liberty by four o'clock; but if I do not come, which is very possible, drive straight here at five or six o'clock in the evening. You will not thus feel so much fatigued, and you can leave this again on Monday, if nothing is neglected by the delay. You can take the money with you for the Correpetitor. Are you aware that this affair of the Correpetitor, including board and lodging, amounts to 2000 florins a year? I can write no more to-day, I can scarcely guide my pen. Show this letter to Reisser.

Your affectionate
FATHER.

*[**Note 1:** I have arranged the following notes to his nephew in their probable succession as to time. Schindler has given some of these in his Biography, but quite at random, and disjointed, without any reliable chronological order.]*

*[**Note 2:** Reisser was Vice-Director of the Polytechnic Institution, where the nephew had been placed for some time. Reisser had also undertaken the office of his co-guardian. Beethoven sometimes writes Reissig.]*

412 - To Dr. Braunhofer.

Baden, May 13, 1825.

MY ESTEEMED FRIEND,--

Doctor. "How does our patient get on?"

Patient. "Still in a bad way, feeling weak and irritable, and I think that at last we must have recourse to stronger medicines, and yet not too violent; surely I might now drink white wine with water, for that deleterious beer is quite detestable. My catarrhal condition is indicated by the following symptoms. I spit a good deal of blood, though probably only from the windpipe. I have constant bleeding from the nose, which has been often the case this winter. There can be no doubt that my digestion is terribly weakened, and in fact my whole system, and, so far as I know my own constitution, my strength will never be recruited by its natural powers."

Doctor. "I will prescribe for you, and soon, very soon, shall your health be restored."

Patient. "How glad I should be to sit down at my writing-table, with some cheerful companions. Reflect on this proposal." Finis.

P.S. I will call on you as soon as I come to town, only tell Carl at what hour I am likely to see you. It would be a good plan to give Carl directions what I am to do. (I took the medicine only once, and have lost it.)

I am, with esteem and gratitude,
Your friend,
BEETHOVEN.

Written on May 11th, 1825, in Baden, Helenenthal, second floor, Anton's-Brücke, near Siechenfeld.

413 - To His Nephew.

Baden, May 17.

MY DEAR SON,--

The weather here is abominable, and the cold greater even than yesterday; so much so that I have scarcely the use of my fingers to write; this is the case, however, only in the mountains, and more especially in Baden. I forgot the chocolate to-day, and am sorry to be obliged to trouble you about it, but all will go better soon. I enclose you 2 florins, to which you must add 15 kreutzers; send it if possible with the post in the afternoon; otherwise I shall have none the day after to-morrow; the people of the house will assist you in this. May God bless you! I begin to write again very tolerably; still, in this most dreary, cold stormy weather, it is almost impossible to have any clear conceptions.

Now as ever,
Your good and loving
FATHER.

414 - To His Nephew.

Noon, 1 o'clock.

MY DEAR SON,--

I merely wish to let you know that the old woman is not yet returned,--why, I cannot tell. Inquire immediately at Höbel's in the Kothgasse, whether the Höbel who belongs to this place set off from Vienna to Baden? It is really so distressing to me to depend on such people, that if life did not possess higher charms, it would be utterly insupportable in my eyes. You no doubt got my yesterday's letter, and the 2 florins for the chocolate. I shall be obliged to drink coffee to-morrow; perhaps after all it is better for me than chocolate, as the prescriptions of this B. [Braunhofer] have been repeatedly wrong. Indeed he seems to me very ignorant, and a blockhead into the bargain; he must have known about the asparagus. Having dined at the inn to-day, I have a threatening of diarrhoea. I have no more white wine, so I must get it from the inn, and such wine too! for which, however, I pay 3 florins! Two days ago the old woman wrote to me that she wished to end her days in an alms-house; perhaps she will not return to me; so be it in God's name! she will always be a wicked old woman. She ought to make arrangements with the person whom she knows of. She wrote to me in a very different strain from that in which she spoke to you on Sunday, and said "that the people refused to give up the bell-pull." Who knows whether she may not have some interest in the matter? She went into town yesterday at six o'clock, and I begged her to make haste back here this forenoon; if she still comes, I must go to town the day after to-morrow. Leave a written message to say when I am to see you.... Write me a few lines immediately. How much I regret troubling you, but you must see that I cannot do otherwise....

Your attached
FATHER.
How distressing to be in such a state here!

To Herr Carl van Beethoven,
Vienna, Alleengasse 72, Karlskirche, 1ter Étage,
at Herr Schlemmer's.

415 - To His Nephew.

MY DEAR SON,--

I sent for the cabinet-maker to-day with the old--witch--to Asinanius'[1] house. Don't forget the paintings, and the things sent in last summer; at all events look for them. I may perhaps come on Saturday; if not, you must come to me on Sunday. May God watch over you, my dear son.

Your attached
FATHER.
I cannot write much. Send me a few words.[2]

*[**Note 1:** It was thus Beethoven named his pseudo-brother.]*

*[**Note 2:** Underneath is written in pencil by another hand, "I shall be at the usual place at three o'clock, s'il vous plait." The whole appears to be afterwards stroked out.]*

416 - To His Nephew.

Do send the chocolate at last by the old woman. If Ramler is not already engaged, he may perhaps drive her over. I become daily thinner, and feel far from well; and no physician, no sympathizing friends! If you can possibly come on Sunday, pray do so; but I have no wish to deprive you of any pleasure, were I only sure that you would spend your Sunday properly away from me.

I must strive to wean myself from everything; if I were only secure that my great sacrifices would bring forth worthy fruits!

Your attached
FATHER.

417 - To His Nephew.

Wednesday, May 17.

MY DEAR SON,--

The old woman is just come, so you need be under no uneasiness; study assiduously and rise early, as various things may occur to you in the morning, which you could do for me. It cannot be otherwise than becoming in a youth, now in his nineteenth year, to combine his duties towards his benefactor and foster-father with those of his education and progress. I fulfilled my obligations towards my own parents. In haste,

Your attached
FATHER.

The old bell-pull is here. The date of my letter is wrong; it is not May the 17th, but the 18th.

418 - To His Nephew.

May 19.

Ask the house agent about a lodging in the Landstrasse, Ungargasse, No. 345, adjoining the Bräuhaus,--four rooms and a kitchen, commanding a view of the adjacent gardens. I hear there are various others too in the

Hauptstrasse. Give a gulden to the house agent in the Ungargasse, to promise me the refusal of the lodgings till Saturday, when, if the weather is not too bad, I mean to come on to fetch you. We must decide to-morrow whether it is to be hired from Michaelmas or now. If I do come on Saturday, take care that I find you at home.

Your attached
FATHER.

419 - To His Nephew.

Say everything that is kind and amiable from me to my esteemed fellow-guardian, Dr. v. Reissig; I feel still too feeble to write to him myself. I hope he will not object to your coming to me here every Saturday evening. You are well aware that I never abused such a permission when you were at Blöchlinger's [see No. 276]. Besides, I feel sure of your intercession in support of my request.

Your attached father,
BEETHOVEN.

420 - To His Nephew.

Baden, May 23.

I have been assured, though as yet it is only a matter of conjecture, that a clandestine intercourse has been renewed between your mother and yourself. Am I doomed again to experience such detestable ingratitude? No! if the tie is to be severed, so be it! By such ingratitude you will incur the hatred of all impartial persons. The expressions my brother made use of yesterday before Dr. Reissig (as he says); and your own with respect to Schönauer (who is naturally adverse to me, the judgment of the Court being the exact reverse of what he desired), were such, that I will not mix myself up with such shameful doings! No! never more!

If you find the Pactum oppressive, then, in God's name, I resign you to His holy keeping! I have done my part, and on this score I do not dread appearing before the Highest of all Judges. Do not be afraid to come to me to-morrow; as yet I only suspect; God grant that those suspicions may not prove true, for to you it would be an incalculable misfortune, with whatever levity my rascally brother, and perhaps your mother also, may treat the matter to the old woman. I shall expect you without fail.

421 - To His Nephew.

Baden, May 31, 1825.

MY DEAR SON,--

I intend to come to town on Saturday, and to return here either on Sunday evening, or early on Monday. I beg you will therefore ask Dr. Bach [advocate] at what hour I can see him, and also fetch the key from brother Bäcker's [a brother-in-law of Johann Beethoven's], to see whether in the room inhabited by my unbrotherly brother, the arrangements are such that I can stay a night there; and if there is clean linen, &c., &c. As Thursday is a holiday, and it is unlikely that you will come here (indeed I do not desire that you should), you may easily execute these two commissions for me. You can let me know the result when I arrive on Saturday. I don't send you money, for if you want any, you can borrow a gulden at home. Moderation is necessary for young people, and you do not appear to pay sufficient attention to this, as you had money without my knowledge, nor do I yet know whence it came. Fine doings! It is not advisable that you should go to the theatre at present, on account of the distraction it causes. The 5 florins procured by Dr. Reissig, I will pay off by instalments, punctually every month. So enough of this! Misled as you have been, it would be no bad thing were you at length to cultivate simplicity and truth, for my heart has been so deeply wounded by your deceitful conduct, that it is difficult to forget it. Even were I disposed to submit like an ox to so hard a yoke without murmuring, if you pursue the same course towards others, you will never succeed in gaining the love of any one. As God is my witness, I can think of nothing but you, and my contemptible brother, and the detestable family that I am afflicted with. May God vouchsafe to listen to my prayer, for never again can I trust you!

Your Father, alas!

Yet fortunately not your Father.

422 - To His Nephew.

Baden, June 9, 1825.

I wish you at least to come here on Sundays. In vain do I ask for an answer. God help you and me!

As ever,

Your attached

FATHER.

I have written to Herr v. Reissig to desire you to come here on Sundays. The calèche leaves his house at six o'clock, from the Kugel, auf der Wieden. You have only to work and study a little in advance, to lose nothing. I regret being obliged to cause you this annoyance; you are to return the same afternoon at five o'clock, with the calèche. Your place is already paid for; you can shave here in the morning, and a shirt and neckcloth will be ready for you, so that you may arrive at the right time.

Farewell. If I reproach you it is not without good cause, and it would be hard to have sacrificed so much, merely to bestow a commonplace man on the world. I hope to see you without fail.

If the intrigues are already matured, say so frankly (and naturally), and you will find one who will always be true to the good cause. The lodging A.

was again advertised in the paper on Tuesday; could you not have arranged about this? You might at all events have done so through some one else, or by writing, if you were at all indisposed. I should much prefer not moving, if I were not compelled to do so. You know my mode of living here, and it is far worse in this cold stormy weather. My continued solitude only still further enfeebles me, and really my weakness often amounts to a swoon. Oh! do not further grieve me, for the scythe of Death will grant me no long delay!

If I could find a good lodging in the Alleengasse, I would at once engage it.

423.

Tuesday Morning.

MY DEAR SON,--

The two patterns, one placed at the top and the other below, each 21 florins, seem to me the best; the landlord can advise you. For the trousers 88--4-1/2. I enclose 62 florins W.W. 30 kreutzers. Give me an exact account of how you spend this money, for it was hard to earn; still it is not worth while, for the sake of a florin a yard, not to select the best material; so choose, or get some one to choose for you, the best of the two at 21 florins. Order the highest quality for your trousers also; remember you ought never to wear your best clothes at home; no matter who comes, you need never be well dressed in the house.[1] The moment you come home change your good clothes, and be at your ease in those set aside for the purpose. Farewell.

Your attached

FATHER.

P.S. The creature went off yesterday and has not returned; we shall see how this turns out. The old beast was determined to be off, being like a restless wild animal devoid of purpose or reason. May Heaven have pity on me! The new cooking began yesterday.

*[**Note 1:** See Weber's narrative in his Biography, Vol. II. 510. "The square Cyclopean figure was attired in a shabby coat with torn sleeves."]*

424 - To His Nephew.

Baden, June 15.

MY DEAR SON,--

I hope you received the 62 florins 30 kreutzers. If you wish to order trousers of the same cloth, do so. You probably chose that at 25 florins, and on such occasions the best quality should not be rejected for the sake of a couple of florins. You may also order two pairs of trousers of the gray cloth. You must let me know the amount of the tailor's bill, &c., &c., which shall be paid by me. "Let not thy left hand know what thy right hand doeth." Such is the sentiment of noble-minded men. You have, alas! only yourself to blame for my being forced to draw your attention to this. Do not forget to call on Riess (??). May Aurora not only awaken you but speed your industry.

Now for my every-day household matters. The maid came indeed, but is not to remain; in the mean time I have spoken pretty plainly to the old woman, so far as it is possible to speak to such people.

But let us say no more of all this bedevilment. My brother Asinanio has written to me. What I find most trying of all is being alone at dinner, and it is really surprising that I can write to you even tolerably from here. Possibly I may come to town on Saturday, and if so you will perhaps drive out here with me at six o'clock in the evening?

Now farewell, my darling! deserve this name. Retain what money you require; anything you want shall be purchased for you when I come in. I embrace you, and hope you will be my good, studious, noble son.

Now as ever, your attached
FATHER.

I should like to know that you received the money safely. Did the Correpetitor come?

425 - To His Nephew.

MY DEAR SON,--

I send you herewith the 90 florins. Get a written receipt from the landlady to prevent all mistakes afterwards; this is the invariable custom with those still under the control of guardians. My wafers are done; cannot you manage to send me a box in some way or other? Acknowledge the receipt of the money at once. God bless you! Do all you possibly can to rid me of that old demon.

Do not involve yourself in any clandestine doings with my brother; above all do nothing clandestine towards me; towards your attached father. Good-night. Farewell! farewell! The old witch and Satan and I?!

426 - To His Nephew.

I rejoice, my dear son, that you take pleasure in this new sphere, and such being the case you must zealously strive to acquire what is necessary for it. I did not recognize your writing; I indeed look only to the sense and meaning, but you must now attain some outward elegance also. If it is too hard a task for you to come here, give it up; but if you can by any possibility do so, I shall rejoice in my desert home to have a feeling heart near me. If you do come, the housekeeper will settle that you leave Vienna at five o'clock, which leaves you ample time for your studies.

I embrace you cordially.
Your attached
FATHER.

P.S. Don't forget to bring the "Morgenblatt" and Ries's letter.[1]

[Note 1: A letter from Ries of this date, in the Fischhof'sche Handschrift, is of sufficient interest to be given here at full length:--

Godesberg, June 9, 1825.

Dearest Beethoven,--I returned a few days ago from Aix-la-Chapelle, and feel the greatest pleasure in telling you that your new Symphony [the 9th] was executed with the most extraordinary precision, and received with the greatest applause. It was a hard nut to crack, and the last day I rehearsed the finale alone for three hours; but I in particular, and all the others, were fully rewarded by the performance. It is a work beside which no other can stand, and had you written nothing but this you would have gained immortality. Whither will you lead us?

As it will interest you to hear something of the performance, I will now briefly describe it. The orchestra and choruses consisted of 422 persons, and many very distinguished people among them. The first day commenced with a new Symphony of mine, and afterwards Handel's Alexander's Feast. The second day began with your new Symphony, followed by the Davide Penitente of Mozart, the overture to the Flaute Magico, and the Mount of Olives. The applause of the public was almost terrific. I had been in Aix-la-Chapelle from the 3d of May on purpose to conduct the rehearsals, and as a mark of the satisfaction and enthusiasm of the public, I was called forward at the close of the performance, when an ode and a laurel crown were presented to me by a lady (a very pretty one too), and at the same moment another poem and a shower of flowers followed from the upper boxes. All was pleasure and contentment, and every one says that this is the finest of the seven Whitsuntide festivals held here.

I cannot sufficiently lament that your other music arrived too late to make use of it. It was indeed utterly impossible to do so. I herewith send you, my dear friend, a check for 40 Louis d'or on Heppenmayer & Co. in Vienna, according to our agreement, and beg you will acknowledge the receipt, that I may settle everything relating to Aix-la-Chapelle.

I am glad that you have not accepted any engagement in England. If you choose to reside there, you must previously take measures to ensure your finding your account in it. From the Theatre alone Rossini got £2500. If the English wish to do anything at all remarkable for you, they must combine, so that it may be well worth your while to go there. You are sure to receive enough of applause, and marks of homage, but you have had plenty of these during your whole life. May all happiness attend you. Dear Beethoven, yours ever,

FERDINAND RIES.]

427 - To His Nephew.

Baden, June 28, 1825.

MY DEAR SON,--

As in this heat you may perhaps wish to bathe, I send you two more florins. You must be careful to take a written receipt from those to whom you pay money; for that errors do occur is proved by the blue cloth, and the three florins for the looking-glass. You are a thorough Viennese, and although I do not expect you to become a W.W. (depreciated Vienna currency), still it is no disgrace at your age to give an exact account of all that you receive, as no one is considered to be of age till five and twenty, and even if you had property of your own, you would be obliged to account for it to your guardian at your present years. Let us not refer to the past; it would be easy to do so, but only cause me pain; at last it would come to this, "You are indeed a first-rate guardian," &c. If you had any depth of feeling you would have acted very differently in most things.

Now as to my domestic rabble; yesterday the kitchenmaid was off again and got a fresh place; the cause is difficult to discover from my old witch, who is now once more all smiles, and no longer persists in declaring that she has incurred any loss from the weekly bills; what do you think of that?

[The last page of this letter is an illegible fragment.]

428 - To His Nephew.

Baden.

MY DEAR GOOD CARL,--

I have just got your letter this evening, and could not help laughing at it. It was not right in the people at Mayence to have acted thus, but since the thing has occurred, it does not signify. Our epoch requires strong minds to scourge those frivolous, contemptible, malicious beings, repulsive as it is to my feelings to cause pain to any man. Besides, I intended a mere jest, and it was far from my intention to let such a thing be printed.[1]

You must ascertain instantly from a magistrate the proper mode of converting the Bank obligations into Rothschild's Austrian Loan, that you may get the authority from a magistrate (not from the Court of those pseudo-guardians!)

Be good and honest; you have here an instance how people rejoice when such men are properly estimated. Be my own dear precious son, and imitate my virtues, but not my faults; still, though man is frail, do not at least have worse defects than those of

Your sincere and fondly attached
FATHER.

Write to me about the conversation on Sunday--it is of the Court, courtly, so you must be on your guard. Holz did not come to-day; whether he is trustworthy I cannot say.

*[**Note 1:** There is no doubt that he alludes to the severe castigation of Haslinger in No. 405 and the canonization of the two others. See also No. 440, which shows that there was something amiss with Haslinger.]*

429 - To His Nephew.

To-day is Friday, to-morrow Saturday.

Here comes Satanas. To-day her raging fury and madness have somewhat subsided, but if she applies to you, refer her to me the day after to-morrow. During the whole week I was forced to submit and to suffer like a saint. Avaunt! such dregs of the people! What a reproach to our civilization to stand in need of a class like this, and to have those whom we despise so constantly near us. Go with her to-morrow as formerly to the Carolin Thor about the Seltzer water; if the small bottles are as genuine as the larger ones, order some of them, but I think the larger size are more likely to be the safest; ce dépend de votre esprit, votre distinction, &c. Now farewell, my dear son; take care to get me the genuine, and not the artificial Seltzer water, and go yourself to see about it, or I might get Heaven knows what! Farewell again, my good fellow; we are well affected towards you, and shall expect you the day after to-morrow at eight o'clock. Breakfast shall be ready for you, if that early meal does not become as usual a late meal. Ah! au diable avec ces grands coquins de neveux, allez-vous en, soyez mon fils, mon fils bien aimé. Adieu; je vous baise, votre père sincère comme toujours.

430 - To His Nephew.

The old goose is the bearer of this. She has given you the quills, and you have again told an untruth. Alas! farewell. I await your report about the book. She is going to-day to Katel, so she will have very little time for her stupid blundering. May the Lord one day deliver me from her! Libera me Domine de illis, &c.

431 - Dear Son, Dear Boy,--

[1]

Do not omit the point about "the happiness." I know from my experience of the late Lichnowsky, that those so-called great personages do not like to see an artist, who is at all events their equal, prosperous. Voilà le même cas, votre Altesse, sometimes in the context V.A. The address "à son Altesse Monseigneur le Prince," &c., &c. We cannot tell whether he may have that weakness or not. A blank sheet ought to follow with my signature. You might add that he must not regard the newspaper trash, the writers of which, if I chose, would loudly trumpet forth my merits. The Quartet did indeed fail the first time that it was played by Schuppanzigh; for on account of his corpulence he requires more time than formerly to decipher a piece at a glance, and many other circumstances concurred in preventing its success, which were indeed predicted by me; for although Schuppanzigh and two others receive pensions from royal personages [Rasumowsky], their quartet-playing is not what it was when all four were in the habit of constantly playing together. On the other hand, it has been six times performed in the most admirable manner by other artists, and received with the greatest applause; it was played twice over in one evening, and then again after supper. A violinist of the name of Böhm means also to give it at his benefit, and I must now let many others have it.

Mention the Grand Quartet in your letter to Peters at Leipzig; lose no time about this, and desire him to send me an early reply. Mischances of this kind cannot well be avoided, and we must appear rather coy. Seal the enclosed letter to my brother and send it to the post. Desire the tailor in the Kärntnerstrasse to get lining for trousers for me, and to make them long and without straps, one pair to be of kerseymere and the other of cloth. The great-coat can be fetched from Wolf's. The shoemaker's shop is in the "Stadt" in the Spiegelgasse, in front when coming from the Graben. His name is Magnus Senn, at the Stadthaus, No. 1093. Call on Hönigstein [a banker] and be candid, that we may really know how this wretch has acted; it would be wise to ascertain this before the letter to Galitzin is sent off. It is probable that something else may be found for you this winter, but we can talk over the matter. Before coming here on Saturday call on Zinbrachen in the Naglergasse about the knives, which you can send at once; the old woman made a fine mess of it! When driving home yesterday I met Clement, Holz, Linke, and Rtschaschek [Rzehatschek] in Neudorf; they had all been to call on me while I was in town. They wish to have the Quartet again. Holz drove straight back here from Neudorf and supped with me in the evening, when I gave him the Quartet to take back with him.

The attachment of genuine artists is not to be despised, and cannot be otherwise than gratifying.

Let me hear from you as soon as you have spoken with Hönigstein; write the dedication of the Overture in C [Op. 124] to Galitzin. If the H.'s undertake to forward it, give it to them, but look sharp about it. God be with you, my dear son; I shall expect a letter from you without fail. May God bless you and me. The end must soon come of your attached father. Good-by, you scamp!

N.B. Do not forget in your letter to Galitzin to mention that the Overture is already announced and about to appear, engraved and dedicated to him.

*[**Note 1:** He refers to Prince Boris Gallizin and the Quartets he had ordered. The production of the first of them in E flat major had been a failure. See No. 399.]*

432 - To His Nephew.

MY DEAR SON,--

Send this letter at once to my pseudo-brother, and add something yourself. It is impossible to permit this to continue any longer; no soup to-day, no beef, no eggs, and at last broiled meat from the inn!

When Holz was with me lately, there was really almost nothing to eat at supper; and such is the woman's bold and insolent behavior, that I have told her to-day I will not suffer her to remain beyond the end of the month. No more to-day. All that is necessary about the magistrate is for me to write a note authorizing you to draw the money, but it would be as well were you to take the opportunity of asking what you are to do about converting the bank shares into a share in Rothschild's Loan. I shall say nothing further, except that I always look on you as my dear son, and one who deserves to be so. Little as I require what nourishes the body, as you know, still the present state of things is really too bad, besides being every moment in danger of being poisoned.

Farewell! Be careful, my dear son, of your health in this heat; I trust you will continue well. Shun all that may enervate or diminish your youthful energies. Farewell! A pleasant talk together would be far better than all this writing. Ever your loving and attached father, who fondly presses you to his heart.

433 - To His Nephew.

MY DEAR SON,--

The enclosed will show you all. Write this letter to Schlesinger.

To ---- Schlesinger, Berlin,

Emporium of Art and Science.

You can couch some things in better terms. I think we may calculate on 80 ducats. If indispensable, delay the letter to Galitzin, but be sure to dispatch the one to Schlesinger on Saturday. I suppose you received the packet? I beg you will bring me some shaving-soap, and at least one pair of razors; the man who grinds them gets 2 florins. You will know if anything is to be paid. Now pray practise economy, for you certainly receive too much money. All in vain--a Viennese will always be a Viennese! I rejoiced when I could assist my poor parents; what a contrast are you in your conduct towards me! Thriftless boy, farewell!

Your attached
FATHER.

Bring the newspaper with you. You have a great deal to do this time. You no doubt will write before Sunday. Do not flatter that wretch ----. He is a miserable, weak-minded fellow. I embrace you. My health is no better.

434 - To His Brother Johann,--Gneixendorf.

Baden, July 13, 1825.

MY WORTHY BROTHER,--

As you have taken such good care of the book, I beg you will take equal care that it be returned to the proprietor here. Another pretty business! As to your wish that I should come to see you, I long ago fully explained myself on that point; so I request that you will never again allude to the subject, for you will find me as immovable as ever. Pray spare me all details, as I am unwilling to repeat what is disagreeable. You are happy, and it is my desire that you should be so; continue thus, for every one is best in his own sphere.

I only once made use of your lodgings, but the baking-oven nearly made me ill, so I did not go again; as I have now a lodging of my own, it is not probable that I shall even once make use of the room you offer me. When you write, be sure to seal your letters, and address them to the care of Carl, in Vienna, as such letters cost a great deal here. I once more urge you to restore the book belonging to the machinist, an dem Graben, for such occurrences are really almost incredible, and place me in no small embarrassment. So the book! the book! to be sent to Carl in Vienna with all possible haste and speed. Farewell, most worthy brother! Yours,

LUDWIG.

435 - To His Nephew.

Baden, July 15.

MY DEAR SON,--

In your letter to Schlesinger don't forget to ask whether Prince Radziwill is in Berlin. As to the 80 ducats, you can also write that they may be paid in Conventionsgulden, at only 4 florins 30 kreutzers to the ducat; but I leave this entirely to yourself, though gold ducats would not be too much from one who has the right of publishing in England and also in France. You must be quite decided too with respect to the four months' bill. A. Mayseder receives 50 ducats for a set of violin variations! Do not fail to call attention to the fact that my bad health and other circumstances constrain me to look more closely after my interests than formerly. Bargaining is odious to me, but it must be so! What are my feelings when I find myself thus alone among these men! Be sure to forward my letter to my brother, that the book may be restored--what a trick! I should have liked, too, to do all I could to benefit my hearing, and here I should have had time to do so. How melancholy to have such a brother! Alas! alas! Farewell! I embrace you from my heart.

Your attached
FATHER.

P.S. Do not be dilatory, and rise early. If you would rather not, pray do not come on Sunday; but at all events write, though not at present, for if you can come we can discuss all matters together.

436 - To His Nephew.

Baden, July 18, Monday.

MY DEAR SON,--

You will see from the enclosure all that you wish to know; only observe moderation. Fortune crowns my efforts, but do not lay the foundation of misery by mistaken notions; be truthful and exact in the account of your expenses, and give up the theatre for the present. Follow the advice of your guide and father; be counselled by him whose exertions and aspirations have always been directed to your moral welfare, though without neglecting your temporal benefit.

This Herr Thal will call on you, and he will also be at Herr Hönigstein's; you can give him the Overture if you think fit. He is to stay three weeks. You may invite him to dine here. Sunday would be best, as a certain scamp comes on that day at an early hour, in a carriage that I will send for him. Pray show some amiability of manner towards this man; art and science form a link between the noblest spirits, and your future vocation[1] by no means exempts you from this. You might take a fiacre and drive to the copyist's if you can spare time. With respect to the transcription of the Quartet, you may tell him that I write very differently now, much more legibly than during my illness; this Quartet must be written out twice, and I can send it at once. I have had the offer of a copyist here, but I don't know what he can do. I should be careful not to be too confidential at first with the Holz Christi, or the splinter of the Holz Christi.

Write to me forthwith. Perhaps the old goose may go to Vienna the day after to-morrow. Farewell! Attend to my advice.

Your attached
FATHER,
Who cordially embraces you.

You may possibly go to D---- with this Herr Thal; do not, however, show too much anxiety about the money.

*[**Note 1:** The nephew had now resolved on a commercial career, and on this account entered the Polytechnic Institution.]*

437 - To His Nephew.

MY DEAR SON,--

So let it be! Bring G----'s letter with you, for I have scarcely read it myself. My Signor Fratello came the day before yesterday with his brother-in-law [see No. 435]--what a contemptible fellow! The old witch, who went almost crazy again yesterday, will bring you the answer about the book from his brother-in-law. If it does not convey a positive certainty on the subject, send this letter at once to the base creature! When Cato exclaimed, with regard to Caesar, "This man and myself!" what can be done in such a case? I don't send the letter, for it will be time enough a couple of days hence. It is too late to-day. I impress my love, as with a seal, on your affectionate attachment to me. If you are likely to miss your work by coming here, then stay where you are.

As ever, your loving and anxious
FATHER.

Three times over:

|: Come soon! :|

438 - To The Copyist.[1]

Read violino 2do--the passage in the first Allegretto in the 1st violin--thus:

So write it in this way; in the first Allegretto, mark the signs of expression in all the four parts:

The notes are all right; so do not misunderstand me.

Now, my good friend, as to your mode of writing--obbligatissimo; but the signs p &c., are shamefully neglected, and often, very often, in the wrong place, which is no doubt owing to haste. For Heaven's sake impress on Kempel [a copyist] to copy everything just as it stands; look carefully over my present corrections, and you will find all that you have to say to him. When • is put over a note, ' is not to take its place, and vice versa. It is not the same thing to write and . The are often purposely placed after the notes. For instance:-- . The ties to be just as they are now placed. It is not synonymous to write  or thus . Such is our will and pleasure! I have passed no less than the whole forenoon to-day, and yesterday afternoon, in correcting these two pieces, and I am actually quite hoarse from stamping and swearing.

In haste, yours,

BEETHOVEN.

Pray excuse me for to-day, as it is just four o'clock. [The close of this letter has not been deciphered by its possessor, who has traced over the hieroglyphics with a pencil; it reads somewhat to this effect, "to go to Carl at four o'clock. We were much amused," &c.]

*[**Note 1:** This letter is evidently written about the same time that the copying of the A minor Quartet (Op. 132) took place, of which the letter treats, and is probably "the enclosure" named in the following note. The corrections, or we ought rather to say revisions, of Beethoven, are all fully and accurately reproduced, at all events in Breitkopf & Härtel's edition.]*

439 - To His Nephew.

Tuesday, August 2.

MY DEAR SON,--

Send the enclosed to-morrow morning (Wednesday) to the post; as it refers to corrections, haste is absolutely necessary. We must have done with this evil old creature! I have scarcely enough to eat, and am forced also to endure the sauciness and insolence of this most malicious old witch--and with such wages too! I think I must ask my pseudo-brother to come, and would be glad to engage again the woman from Winter's, in the Kothgasse, who at least knew how to cook.

Write me a few lines to-morrow, and direct here. I send you another florin. Do not neglect your bathing; continue well, and guard against illness. Spend your money on good objects alone. Be my dear son! What a frightful discord would it be, were you to prove false to me, as many persons maintain that you already are! May God bless you!

Your attached

FATHER.

N.B. Send off the letter to-morrow (Wednesday). I have heard nothing as yet of the knives, and my made pens also begin to fail.

440 - To His Nephew.

Baden, August

MY DEAR SON,--

I am in mortal anxiety about the Quartet--namely, the third, fourth, fifth, and sixth parts, that Holz took away, while the first bars of the third movement have been left here; the number of these sheets is 13. I hear nothing of Holz. I wrote to him yesterday, and he is not usually remiss in writing. What a sad business it will be if he has lost it! He drinks hard, entre nous. Tranquillize me on this point as quickly as possible. You can find out Linke's lodgings from Haslinger; he was here to-day and very friendly, and brought some of the sheets and other things, and begged hard for the new quartets. Never interfere in this kind of business; it can only lead to what is unpleasant. For Heaven's sake pacify me about the Quartet--a serious loss. The sketch is only written on small fragments of paper, and I could not manage to write out the whole exactly from these.

Your attached
FATHER.

I must remind you that next Sunday and Monday are holidays, so that you may arrange accordingly. On this occasion you could perhaps, when I come in, return with me here on Saturday evening, which would give you the whole of Sunday morning to yourself.

441 - To Zmeskall.

1825.

MY GOOD FRIEND,--

I had scarcely got home when I bethought me of the stuff I may have written yesterday. Give the enclosed to Kuhlau; you know all the rest. Write to me as soon as possible, or come here, next Thursday being a holiday, but write beforehand. Ask if the cook understands anything about game, that she may take the command of my game preserves for me. As to Carl, it would be better for him to tell me about it at the Atrapper at Rosen. All this prestissimo! As for my friendship, think of me always as Cantum firmum. Farewell!

Ever your friend,
BEETHOVEN.

442 - To Herr Friedrich Kuhlau.

Baden, September 3, 1825.

I must admit that the champagne went a little to my head yesterday, and I learned once more from experience, that such things rather prostrate than promote my energies; for, though able to respond fluently at the moment, still I can no longer recall what I wrote yesterday.

Sometimes bear in mind your attached

BEETHOVEN.

443 - To His Nephew.

September 6, 1825.

MY DEAR SON,--

I see perfectly well how troublesome it would be for you all to come here; we must therefore make an appointment to meet every Friday at Schlesinger's, when I will come to town; for, in case any thing goes amiss, I must be present. This is the best plan, and settles the affair. He was here yesterday, and said that he would pay for the Quintet as soon as you sent it to him.

It will be enough if they play the new one only, but you can judge what is best. If they prefer Thursday, I can be present then. Only see that they come to an arrangement as quickly as possible, so that the money may be transmitted to Peters in Leipzig, to whom, however, you must on no account allude. Schlesinger scarcely expects to be still in Vienna on Sunday; haste is therefore necessary. The ducats must be in gold; mention, as a precedent, that others do this.

Be sure to write to me by the old woman to-day. All I want is a rehearsal, to see whether corrections are required. Make no delays, and take care that the old woman sets off in good time. The best plan would be to fix where I am to come to in town every Friday for rehearsals. If Schlesinger has brought you the Quartet (the first), pray stand on no ceremony, for it is clear he means to pay.

Your letter has this moment come. So Holz is not to be here till Thursday, and who can tell whether even this is certain? Your letter changes everything, as Friday is now decided on. Holz can inform me whether we meet here or in Vienna. Our main point now is with Schlesinger, for we must delay no longer. If he is only waiting for the rehearsal, he certainly shall not have it. He said yesterday that he would not publish the quartets here; I told him it was a matter of entire indifference to me. May God bless you and keep you!

Your attached

FATHER.

444 - To His Nephew.

September.

MY DEAR SON,--

Do not forget to give Tobias [Haslinger] the receipt together with the money. The gentleman ought to have come a little sooner; but as the affair stands, you must do as he advises. I do not wish now that you should come to me on the 19th of September. It is better to finish your studies. God has never yet forsaken me, and no doubt some one will be found to close my eyes. The whole thing seems to me to have been some artful collusion, in which my brother (pseudo) has played a part. I also know that you have no pleasure now in coming to me--which is only natural, for my atmosphere is too pure for you. Last Sunday you again borrowed 1 florin 15 kreutzers from the housekeeper, from a mean old kitchen wench,--this was already forbidden,--and it is the same in all things. I could have gone on wearing the out-of-doors coat for two years--to be sure I have the shabby custom of putting on an old coat at home--but Herr Carl! What a disgrace it would be! and why should he do so? Herr Ludwig van Beethoven's money-bags are expressly for this purpose.

You had better not come next Sunday, for true harmony and concord can never exist with conduct such as yours. Why such hypocrisy? Avoid it, and you will then become a better man, and not require to be deceitful nor untruthful, which will eventually benefit your moral character. Such is the impression you have made on my mind--for what avail even the most gentle reproofs? They merely serve to embitter you. But do not be uneasy; I shall continue to care for you as much as ever. What feelings were aroused in me when I again found a florin and 15 kreutzers charged in the bill!

Do not send any more such flimsy notes, for the housekeeper can see through them in the light. I have just received this letter from Leipzig, but I don't mean to send the Quartet yet; we can talk of this on Sunday. Three years ago I only asked 40 ducats for a quartet; we must therefore refer to the exact words you have written.

Farewell! He who, though he did not give you life, has certainly provided for it, and above all striven to perfect your mental culture, and been more than a father to you, earnestly implores you to pursue steadily the only true path to all that is good and right. Farewell!

Bring back the letter with you on Sunday.

Your attached and kind

FATHER.

445 - To Herr Von Schlesinger.

Vienna, September 26, 1825.

My worthy friend, I wish you the loveliest bride! And I take this opportunity of asking you to present my compliments to Herr Marx, in Berlin, and beg him not to be too hard on me, and sometimes to allow me to slip out at the backdoor.

Yours,

BEETHOVEN.

446 - To His Nephew.

Baden, October 4.

MY DEAR SON,--

Like the sage Odysseus, I know the best course to take; if you come on Saturday, you need not fear the cold, for a portion of the old window-shutters is still here, with which we can protect ourselves. I hope also to get rid of my cold and catarrh here; at the same time this place is a great risk in my rheumatic condition, for wind, or rather hurricanes, still prevail here. As to Biedermann, you must inquire whether Schlesinger gave him a commission; for if this be not the case, we ought to write at once to Peters. You could scarcely write to me to-day, but I hope to hear from you to-morrow, and to see you positively on Saturday. I wish you never may have cause to feel ashamed of your want of love for me; if I alone suffer, what matters it? I wish and hope that all the pretexts you made here to go into Vienna may prove true.

Rest assured that you may at all times expect every possible kindness from me, but can I hope for the same from you? When you see me irritable, ascribe it solely to my great anxiety on your account, for you are exposed to many dangers. I hope at all events to get a letter from you to-morrow; do not cause me uneasiness, but think of my sufferings. I ought not, properly, to have any such apprehensions, but what sorrow have I not already experienced?!

As ever, your attached
FATHER.

Remember that I am all alone here, and subject to sudden illness. [On the outside:] N'oubliez pas de demander des quittances, et donnez-moi aussi vite que possible des nouvelles.

447 - To His Nephew.

MY DEAR SON,--

Say no more! only come to my arms; not one harsh word shall you hear! For God's sake do not bring misery on your own head. You shall be received as lovingly as ever. We can discuss in a friendly manner what is to be done and settled as to the future. I pledge my word of honor you shall meet with no reproaches from me, which, indeed, could no longer avail. You need expect only the most affectionate care and assistance from me. Only come! Come to the faithful heart of--
Your father,
BEETHOVEN.
Volti sub.

Set off the moment you receive this letter. Si vous ne viendrez pas, vous me tuerez sûrement. Lisez la lettre et restez à la maison chez vous. Venez embrasser votre père, vous vraiment adonné. Soyez assuré que tout cela restera entre nous. For God's sake come home to-day, for we cannot tell what risks you run,--hasten,--hasten to me!

448 - To His Nephew.

October 5.

DEAR AND MUCH-BELOVED SON,--

I have just received your letter. I was a prey to anguish, and resolved to hurry into Vienna myself this very day. God be praised! this is not necessary; follow my advice, and love and peace of mind, as well as worldly happiness, will attend us, and you can then combine an inward and spiritual existence with your outer life. But it is well that the former should be esteemed superior to the latter. Il fait trop froid. So I am to see you on Saturday? Write to say whether you come early or in the evening, that I may hasten to meet you. I embrace and kiss you a thousand times over, not my lost, but my new-born son.

I wrote to Schlemmer; do not take it amiss, but my heart is still too full [a piece is here torn away]. Live! and my care of the son I have found again will show only love on the part of your father. [On the cover:] Ayez la bonté de m'envoyer a lucifer-match bottle and matches from Rospini, ou en portez avec vous, puisque de celle de Kärnthnerthor on ne veut pas faire usage.

449 - To His Nephew.

Immediate. Baden, October 14.

I write in the greatest haste to say, that even if it rains, I shall certainly come in to-morrow forenoon; be sure, therefore, that I find you at home.

I rejoice at the thoughts of seeing you again, and if you detect any heavy clouds lowering, do not attribute them to deliberate anger, for they will be wholly chased away by your promise to strive more earnestly after the true and pure happiness, based on active exertion. Something hovered before me in my last letter, which though perhaps not quite justly yet called forth a dark mood; this, after all that has passed, was indeed very possible; still who would not rejoice when the transgressor returns to the right path?--and this I hope I shall live to see. I was especially pained by your coming so late on Sunday, and hurrying away again so early. I mean to come in to-morrow with the joiner and to send off these old hags; they are too bad for anything. Until the other housekeeper arrives, I can make use of the joiner. More of this when we meet, and I know you will think I am right. Expect me then to-morrow without fail, whether it rains or not.

Your loving
FATHER,
Who fondly embraces you.

450 - To the Abbé Maximilian Stadler.

February 6, 1826.

REVEREND AND HONORED SIR,--

You have really done well in rendering justice to the manes of Mozart by your inimitable pamphlet, which so searchingly enters into the matter [the Requiem], and you have earned the gratitude of the lay and the profane, as well as of all who are musical, or have any pretensions to be so. To bring a thing of this kind forward as H.W.[1] has done, a man must either be a great personage, or a nonentity. Be it remembered also that it is said this same person has written a book on composition, and yet has ascribed to Mozart such passages as the following:--

and has added such things as,--

as samples of his own composition! H.W.'s astonishing knowledge of harmony and melody recall the old composers of the Empire,--Sterkel, [illegible,] Kalkbrenner (the father), André, &c.

Requiescant in pace! I especially thank you, my dear friend, for the pleasure you have conferred on me by your pamphlet. I have always accounted myself one of Mozart's greatest admirers, and shall continue to be so to my last breath. I beg, venerable sir, for your blessing, and I am, with sincere esteem and veneration, yours,

BEETHOVEN.

*[**Note 1**: Gottfried Weber, the well-known theorist, who was one of those engaged in the dispute as to the genuineness of Mozart's Requiem.]*

451 - To Gottfried Weber

April 3, 1826.

Holz tells me that it is your intention to publish a larger size of the engraving representing Handel's monument, in St. Peter's Church in London. This affords me extreme pleasure, independent of the fact that I was the person who suggested this. Accept my thanks beforehand.

I am your obedient

BEETHOVEN.

452 - To Herr Probst, Music Publisher,--Leipzig.

Vienna, June 3, 1826.

SIR,--

I always consider myself in some degree bound to make you the offer of my compositions when it is possible to do so. I am at this moment more at liberty than usual. I was obliged to give my minor works to those who took the greater ones also, as without the former they refused to accept the latter. So far as I remember, however, you wished to have nothing to do with the greater works. In this view, I offer you an entirely new Quartet for two violins, viola and violoncello; you must not, however, be surprised at my demanding the sum of 80 gold ducats for it. I assure you, upon my honor, that the same sum has been remitted to me for several quartets. I must request you, in any event, to write to me on this point as soon as possible. Should you accept my offer, I beg you will send the money to some bank here, where I can receive it on delivery of the work. If the reverse be the case, I shall equally expect an immediate reply, as other publishers have already made me offers. I have also the following trifles ready, with which I can supply you. A Serenade-congratulatory-Minuet, and an Entr'acte, both for a full orchestra,--the two for 20 gold ducats. In the hope of a speedy answer,

I am, sir, your obedient

BEETHOVEN.

453 - To Stephan V. Breuning.[1]

MY DEAR AND MUCH-LOVED STEPHAN,--

May our temporary estrangement be forever effaced by the portrait I now send. I know that I have rent your heart. The emotion which you cannot fail now to see in mine has sufficiently punished me for it. There was no malice towards you in my heart, for then I should be no longer worthy of your friendship. It was passion both on your part and on mine; but mistrust was rife within me, for people had come between us, unworthy both of you and of me.

My portrait[2] was long ago intended for you; you knew that it was destined for some one--and to whom could I give it with such warmth of heart as to you, my faithful, good, and noble Stephan?

Forgive me for having grieved you; but I did not myself suffer less when I no longer saw you near me. I then first keenly felt how dear you were, and ever will be to my heart. Surely you will once more fly to my arms as you formerly did.

*[**Note 1:** Schindler places this letter in the summer of 1826, when his nephew attempted self-destruction in Baden, which reduced Beethoven to the most miserable state of mind, and brought afresh to his recollection those dear friends of his youth, whom he seemed almost to have forgotten in the society of Holz and his colleagues. Schindler states that the more immediate cause of this estrangement was Breuning having tried to dissuade him from adopting his nephew. Dr. v. Breuning in Vienna is of opinion that the reunion of the two old friends had already occurred in 1825, or even perhaps at an earlier period. I am not at present capable of finally deciding on this discrepancy, but I believe the latter assertion to be correct.]*

*[**Note 2:** Schindler says, "It was Stieler's lithograph, which the maestro had previously sent to Dr. Wegeler." See No. 459.]*

454 - To Stephan von Breuning.

MY BELOVED FRIEND,--

You are harassed by work, and so am I--besides, I am still far from well. I would have invited you to dinner ere this, but I have been obliged to entertain people whose most highly prized author is the cook, and not finding his interesting productions at home, they hunt after them in the kitchens and cellars of others [Holz for instance]. Such society would not be very eligible for you, but all this will soon be altered. In the mean time do not buy Czerny's "School for the Pianoforte;"[1] for in a day or two I expect to get some information about another. Along with the "Journal des Modes" that I promised to your wife, I also send something for your children. I can always regularly transmit you the journal--you have only to express your wish on any point, for me to comply with it at once.

I am, with love and esteem, your friend,
BEETHOVEN.

I hope we shall soon meet.

*[**Note 1:** Czerny, The Vienna Pianoforte Teacher; or, theoretical and practical mode of learning how to play the piano skilfully and beautifully in a short time by a new and easy method. Vienna: Haslinger. See No. 455.]*

455 - To Stephan V. Breuning

MY DEAR GOOD FRIEND,--

I can at length realize my boast, and send you Clement's long-promised "Pianoforte School" for Gerhard [Breuning's eldest son]. If he makes the use of it that I advise, the results cannot fail to be good. I shall see you very shortly now, and cordially embrace you.

Your
BEETHOVEN.

456 - To Carl Holz.

[1]

TESTIMONIAL FOR C. HOLZ.

Vienna, August 30, 1826.

I am happy to give my friend Carl Holz the testimonial he wishes, namely, that I consider him well fitted to write my Biography hereafter, if indeed I may presume to think that this will be desired. I place the most implicit confidence in his faithfully transmitting to posterity what I have imparted to him for this purpose.

LUDWIG VAN BEETHOVEN.

*[**Note 1:** Carl Holz ceded his rights to Dr. Gassner, who however died in 1851 without having completed any biography of Beethoven. In the maestro's bequest, which Gassner's widow was so kind as to show me, there was nothing new (at least to me) except two letters included in this collection and a couple of anecdotes. Schindler also states that Beethoven subsequently repented of the authority he had given Holz and declared he did so too hastily.]*

457 - To Carl Holz.

Both the gentlemen were here, but they have been admonished on every side to observe the most strict secrecy with regard to the Order. Haslinger declares that in this respect you are a son of the deceased Papageno. Prenez garde!

I told Carl to-day it was definitively settled that he could not quit the hospital except with you or me. I dine at home to-morrow, so I shall be very glad if you can come. As you have no official work to-morrow you might arrive later, but it is very necessary that you should come. Portez-vous bien, Monsieur terrible amoureux.[1]

Your indeclinable friend,

BEETHOVEN.

*[**Note 1:** This letter contains all kinds of dashes and flourishes, which prove that the maestro was in his happiest mood when he wrote it. His nephew was at that time in the hospital, probably owing to his attempt at suicide.]*

458 - To the King of Prussia.

YOUR MAJESTY,--

One of the greatest pieces of good fortune of my life is your Majesty having graciously permitted me respectfully to dedicate my present work [the 9th Symphony] to you.

Your Majesty is not only the father of your subjects, but also a patron of art and science; and how much more precious is your gracious permission to me, from being myself so fortunate as to be numbered among your subjects, being a citizen of Bonn.

I beg your Majesty will vouchsafe to accept this work as a slender token of the profound admiration with which I regard your virtues.

I am, your Majesty's obedient humble servant,

LUDWIG VAN BEETHOVEN.

459 - To Wegeler.

Vienna, October 7, 1826.

MY OLD AND BELOVED FRIEND,--

I really cannot express the pleasure your letter and that of your Lorchen caused me. An answer speedy as an arrow's flight ought indeed to have responded, but I am always rather indolent about writing, because I think that the better class of men know me sufficiently without this. I often compose the answer in my head, but when I wish to write it down I generally throw aside the pen, from not being able to write as I feel. I recall all the kindness you have ever shown me; for example, your causing my room to be whitewashed, which was an agreeable surprise to me. It was just the same with all the Breuning family. Our separation was in the usual course of things; each striving to pursue and to attain his object; while at the same time the everlasting and immutable principles of good still held us closely united. I cannot unfortunately write so much to you to-day as I could wish, being confined to bed,[1] so I limit my reply to some points in your letter.

You write that in some book I am declared to be the natural son of the late King of Prussia; this was mentioned to me long ago, but I have made it a rule never either to write anything about myself, or to answer anything written by others about me. I therefore gladly devolve on you the duty of making known to the world the respectability of my parents, and especially that of my mother.

You write to me about your son. There is no possible doubt that when he comes here he will find a friend and a father in me, and whenever it may be in my power to serve or to assist him, I will gladly do so.

I still have the silhouette of your Lorchen, by which you will see how dear to me to this hour are all those who were kind and loving to me in the days of my youth. As to my diploma, I may briefly state that I am an Honorary Member of the Royal Academy of Science in Sweden [see No. 338] and in Amsterdam, and that I have been presented with the Honorary Citizenship of Vienna. A Dr. Spiecker lately took with him to Berlin my last Grand Symphony with Choruses; it is dedicated to the King, and I wrote the dedication with my own hand. I had previously applied at the Embassy for permission to dedicate the work to the King, which has now been accorded.[2] By desire of Dr. Spiecker I gave him the manuscript I had myself corrected, and with my own amendments, to present to the King, as it is to be deposited in the Royal Library. I received a hint at the time about the second class of the Order of the

Red Eagle; I do not know what the result may be, for I have never sought such distinctions, though in these days for many reasons they would not be unwelcome to me. Besides, my maxim has always been,--Nulla dies sine linea; and if I allow my Muse to slumber, it is only that she may awake with fresh vigor. I hope yet to usher some great works into the world, and then to close my earthly career like an old child somewhere among good people.[3] You will soon receive some music through the Brothers Schott, in Mayence. The portrait which I now send you is indeed an artistic masterpiece, but not the last that has been taken of me. I must tell you further, what I know you will rejoice to hear, with regard to marks of distinction. The late King of France sent me a medal with the inscription, Donné par le Roi à M. Beethoven, accompanied by a very polite letter from le premier gentilhomme du Roi, le Duc de Châtres.

My beloved friend, excuse my writing more to-day, for the remembrance of the past has deeply affected me, and not without many tears have I written this letter. The oftener you write the more pleasure will you confer on me. There can be no question on either side as to our friendship, so farewell. I beg you will embrace your dear children and your Lorchen in my name, and think of me when you do so. May God be with you all.

As ever, your attached friend, with sincere esteem,
BEETHOVEN.

*[**Note 1:** On which account this letter is dictated, and only signed by Beethoven, who was at that time at his brother's house in the country--Gneixendorf, near Krems, on the Danube.]*

*[**Note 2:** In consequence of his application to the King of Prussia to subscribe to his Mass, of which he had sent the MS., Beethoven received the following intimation:--*

To the Composer Ludwig van Beethoven.

Berlin, Nov. 25, 1826.

"It gave me great pleasure to receive your new work, knowing the acknowledged value of your compositions. I thank you for having sent it to me, and present you with a ring of brilliants, as a token of my sincere appreciation.

"FRIEDRICH WILHELM."

Schindler adds that the stones in the ring were false, and casts a suspicion of fraud on the Chancery Director of that day, W----.]

*[**Note 3:** It was during those weeks that he wrote the second Finale to the B. flat major Quartet, Op. 130, little anticipating that this was to be his "Swan song."]*

460 - To Tobias Haslinger.[1]

No time is left to-day for further words and vocalization. I beg you will at once deliver the enclosed letter. Pray forgive my causing you this trouble; but, as you are the owner of an artistic post-office, it is scarcely possible not to take advantage of this.

You will perceive that I am now at Gneixendorf. The name sounds like the breaking of an axletree. The air is healthy. The memento mori must be applied to all else. Most marvellous and best of all Tobiases, we salute you in the name of the arts and poets!

I remain yours,
BEETHOVEN.

*[**Note 1:** The music alone and the words "I remain" at the close, are in Beethoven's writing. The rest is probably written by his nephew, with whom he had been obliged to take refuge in the house of his odious brother near Krems, because the police had intimated to the young delinquent that he must leave Vienna. See No. 435 on the subject of Beethoven's repugnance to live in his brother's family circle, whose ignoble wife treated the gray-haired and suffering maestro as badly as possible.]*

461 - To Tobias Haslinger.

GNEIXENDORF, October 13, 1826.

BEST OF ALL TOBIASES,--*[Here follow eight bars of music.]* We are writing to you from the castle of our Signor Fratello. I must again intrude on you by the polite request to post the two enclosed letters without delay.

I will repay you for the time I kept the "School for the Pianoforte" and all the other expenses as soon as I return to Vienna. I am staying here longer, owing to the weather being so fine, and also not having gone to the country at all during the summer. A quartet[1] for Schlesinger is already finished; only I don't know which is the safest way to send it to you, that you may give it to Tendler and Manstein and receive the money in return. Schlesinger will probably not make the remittance in gold, but if you can contrive that I should get it, you would very much oblige me, as all my publishers pay me in gold. Besides, my worthy Tobiasserl, we stand in need of money, and it is by no means the same thing whether we have money or not. If you get a sight of Holz make sure of him, and nail him at once. The passion of love has so violently assailed him that he has almost taken fire, and some one jestingly wrote that Holz was a son of the deceased Papageno.

Most astounding, most admirable, and most unique of all Tobiases, farewell! If not inconvenient, pray write me a few lines here. Is Dr. Spiecker still in Vienna? I am, with highest consideration and fidelity,

Yours,
BEETHOVEN.

*[**Note 1:** Probably the one in F, Op. 135.]*

462 - To Carl Holz.

Dec. 1826.

YOUR OFFICIAL MAJESTY,--

I wrote to you on my arrival here a few days ago, but the letter was mislaid; I then became so unwell that I thought it best to stay in bed. I shall therefore be very glad if you will pay me a visit. You will find it less inconvenient, because every one has left Döbling to go to town. I only add, in conclusion,[1]

As ever, your friend,
BEETHOVEN.

*[**Note 1:** Here Beethoven's own writing begins. The slight indisposition that he mentions, in the course of a few days became a serious illness, the result of which was dropsy, and from this the maestro was doomed never to recover. Indeed from that time he never again left his bed.]*

463 - To Dr. Bach.[1]

Vienna, Wednesday, Jan. 3, 1827.

MY RESPECTED FRIEND,--

I hereby declare, at my decease, my beloved nephew, Carl van Beethoven, sole heir of all my property, and of seven bank shares in particular, as well as any ready money I may be possessed of. If the law prescribes any modifications in this matter, pray endeavor to regulate these as much as possible to his advantage.

I appoint you his curator, and beg that, together with Hofrath Breuning, his guardian, you will supply the place of a father to him.

God bless you! A thousand thanks for all the love and friendship you have shown towards me.

LUDWIG VAN BEETHOVEN.

*[**Note 1:** The signature alone is in Beethoven's writing.]*

464 - To Wegeler.

Vienna, February 17, 1827.

MY OLD AND WORTHY FRIEND,--

I received your second letter safely through Breuning. I am still too feeble to answer it, but you may be assured that its contents were most welcome and agreeable to me.[1] My convalescence, if indeed I may call it such, makes very slow progress, and there is reason to suspect that a fourth operation will be necessary, although the medical men have not as yet decided on this. I arm myself with patience, and reflect that all evil leads to some good. I am quite surprised to find from your last letter that you had not received mine. From this one you will see that I wrote to you on the 10th of December last. It is the same with the portrait, as you will perceive from the date, when you get it. "Frau Steffen spake the word:" Michael Steffen insisted on sending them by some private hand; so they have been lying here until this very day, and really it was a hard matter to get them back even now. You will receive the portrait by the post, through the Messrs. Schott, who have also sent you the music.

How much is there that I would fain say to you to-day; but I am too weak,[2] so I can only embrace you and your Lorchen in spirit. With true friendship and attachment to you and yours,

Your old and faithful friend,

BEETHOVEN.

*[**Note 1:** Wegeler had reminded him of Blumenauer, who, after being operated on for dropsy, lived for many years in perfect health. He at the same time suggested to him the plan of going with him in the ensuing summer to one of the Bohemian baths, proposing to travel by a circuitous route to the Upper Rhine, and from thence to Coblenz.]*

*[**Note 2:** Beethoven's last letter to Wegeler. The signature alone is his.]*

465 - To Sir George Smart, London.

Feb. 22, 1827.

I remember that some years ago the Philharmonic Society proposed to give a concert for my benefit. This prompts me to request you, dear sir, to say to the Philharmonic Society that if they be now disposed to renew their offer it would be most welcome to me. Unhappily, since the beginning of December I have been confined to bed by dropsy,--a most wearing malady, the result of which cannot yet be ascertained. As you are already well aware, I live entirely by the produce of my brains, and for a long time to come all idea of writing is out of the question. My salary is in itself so small, that I can scarcely contrive to defray my half-year's rent out of it. I therefore entreat you kindly to use all your influence for the furtherance of this project,--your generous sentiments towards me convincing me that you will not be offended by my application. I intend also to write to Herr Moscheles on this subject, being persuaded that he will gladly unite with you in promoting my object. I am so weak that I can no longer write, so I only dictate this. I hope, dear sir, that you will soon cheer me by an answer, to say whether I may look forward to the fulfilment of my request.

In the mean time, pray receive the assurance of the high esteem with which I always remain, &c., &c.

466 - To Herr Moscheles.

Vienna, Feb. 22, 1827.

DEAR MOSCHELES,--

I feel sure that you will not take amiss my troubling you as well as Sir G. Smart (to whom I enclose a letter) with a request. The matter is briefly this. Some years since, the London Philharmonic Society made me the handsome offer to give a concert in my behalf. At that time I was not, God be praised! so situated as to render it necessary for me to take advantage of this generous proposal. Things are, however, very different with me now, as for fully three months past I have been entirely prostrated by that tedious malady, dropsy. Schindler encloses a letter with further details. You have long known my circumstances, and are aware how, and by what, I live: a length of time must elapse before I can attempt to write again, so that, unhappily, I might be reduced to actual want. You have not only an extensive acquaintance in London, but also the greatest influence with the Philharmonic; may I beg you, therefore, to exercise it, so far as you can, in prevailing on the Society to resume their former intention, and to carry it soon into effect.

The letter I enclose to Sir Smart is to the same effect, as well as one I already sent to Herr Stumpff.[1] I beg you will yourself give the enclosed letter to Sir Smart, and unite with him and all my friends in London in furthering my object. Your sincere friend,

BEETHOVEN.

*[**Note 1:** Stumpff, a Thuringian maker of harps, came to Vienna in 1824, recommended to our maestro by Andreas Streicher in a letter of Sept. 24, in these words:--"The bearer of this is Herr Stumpff, an excellent German, who has lived for thirty-four years in London. The sole reason of his going to Baden is to see you, my revered Beethoven, the man of whom Germany is so proud. Pray receive him in a kind and friendly manner, as beseems the saint to whose shrine the pious pilgrim has made so long a journey." In 1826 he presented Beethoven with the English edition of Handel's works in 40 folio volumes, which the maestro constantly studied during his last illness. Gerhard v. Breuning, when a youth of fourteen, either held up the separate volumes for him, or propped them against the wall.]*

467 - To Schindler.

The end of February, 1827.

When we meet we can discuss the mischance that has befallen you. I can send you some person without the smallest inconvenience. Do accept my offer; it is, at least, something. Have you had no letters from Moscheles or Cramer? There will be a fresh occasion for writing on Wednesday, and once more urging my project. If you are still indisposed at that time, one of my people can take the letter, and get a receipt from the post-office.

Vale et fave. I need not assure you of my sympathy with your misfortune. Pray allow me to supply board for you in the mean time. I offer this from my heart. May Heaven preserve you! Your sincere friend,

BEETHOVEN.

468 - To Baron Von Pasqualati. [1]

March 6, 1827.

MY MUCH-ESTEEMED OLD FRIEND,--

My warmest thanks for the kind present you have sent me for the benefit of my health; as soon as I have found what wine is most suitable for me I will let you know, but not abuse your kindness. I like the compote much, and shall again apply to you for some. Even this costs me an effort. Sapienti pauca.

Your grateful friend,
BEETHOVEN.

*[**Note 1:** Traced in feeble and trembling characters. Some other hand has written on it, "March 6, 1827."]*

469 - To Baron Von Pasqualati.

MY ESTEEMED FRIEND,--

I beg you will send me some more of the cherry compote, but without lemons, and quite simple. I should also like a light pudding, almost liquid, my worthy cook not being very experienced in invalid diet. I am allowed to drink champagne, and I wish you would send me for to-day a champagne glass with it. Now, as to wine, Malfatti wished me to drink moselle, but declared that no genuine moselle could be got here; so he gave me several bottles of Krumbholzkirchner, [1] deeming this best for my health, as no really good moselle is to be had. Pray forgive my troubling you, and ascribe it chiefly to my helpless condition.

I am, with much esteem, your friend,
BEETHOVEN.

*[**Note 1:** Gumpoldskirchner--a celebrated and generous Austrian wine.]*

470 - To Sir George Smart,--London.

March 6, 1827.

DEAR SIR,--

I make no doubt that you have already received through Herr Moscheles my letter of February 22, but as I found your address by chance among my papers, I do not hesitate to write direct to yourself, to urge my request once more on you in the strongest terms.

I do not, alas! even up to the present hour, see any prospect of the termination of my terrible malady; on the contrary, my sufferings, and consequently my cares, have only increased. I underwent a fourth operation on the 27th of February, and possibly fate may compel me to submit to this a fifth time, and perhaps oftener. If this goes on, my illness will certainly continue one half the summer, and in that case, what is to become of me? How am I to subsist until I can succeed in arousing my decayed powers, and once more earn my living by my pen? But I do not wish to plague you by fresh complaints; so I only refer you to my letter of the 22d February, and entreat you to use all your influence with the Philharmonic Society to carry now into execution their former proposal of a concert for my benefit.

471 - To Baron Von Pasqualati.

MY WORTHY FRIEND,--

I am still confined to my room; be so good, therefore, as to tell me, or rather, I should say, write to me, the name of the person who values this house, and where he is to be found. If you have any Muterhall [?] medicine I beg you will think of your poor Austrian musician and citizen of the guild.
BEETHOVEN.

472 - To Baron von Pasqualati.

[1]
March 14, 1827.

MY ESTEEMED FRIEND,--

Many thanks for the dish you sent me yesterday, which will suffice for today also. I am allowed to have game; and the doctor said that fieldfares were very wholesome for me. I only tell you this for information, as I do not want them to-day. Forgive this stupid note, but I am exhausted from a sleepless night. I embrace you, and am, with much esteem, your attached friend.

*[**Note 1:** In a tremulous hand,--"March 14, 1827."]*

473 - To Herr Moscheles.

Vienna, March 14, 1827.

MY DEAR MOSCHELES,--

I recently heard, through Herr Lewisey, [1] that in a letter to him of the 10th February, you had made inquiries as to the state of my health, about which such various rumors have been circulated. Although I cannot possibly doubt that you have by this time received my letter of February 22d, which explains all you wish to know, still I cannot resist thanking you for your sympathy with my sad condition, and again imploring you to attend to the request contained in my first letter. I feel already certain that, in conjunction with Sir Smart and other friends, you are sure to succeed in obtaining a favorable result for me from the Philharmonic Society. I wrote again to Sir Smart also on the subject.

I was operated on for the fourth time on the 27th of February, and now symptoms evidently exist which show that I must expect a fifth operation. What is to be done? What is to become of me if this lasts much longer? Mine has indeed been a hard doom; but I resign myself to the decrees of fate, and only constantly pray to God that His holy will may ordain that while thus condemned to suffer death in life, I may be shielded from want. The Almighty will give me strength to endure my lot, however severe and terrible, with resignation to His will.

So once more, dear Moscheles, I commend my cause to you, and shall anxiously await your answer, with highest esteem. Hummel is here, and has several times come to see me.

Your friend,
BEETHOVEN.

*[**Note 1:** Schindler mentions, on Beethoven's authority, that this gentleman translated Beethoven's letters to Smart into English, which his nephew had previously done.]*

474. [1]

TO SCHINDLER.--
March 17, 1827.

WONDERFUL! WONDERFUL! WONDERFUL!--

Both the learned gentlemen are defeated, and I shall be saved solely by Malfatti's skill! You must come to me for a few minutes without fail this forenoon.

Yours,
BEETHOVEN.

*[**Note 1:** Schindler dates this note March 17, 1827, and says that these are the last lines Beethoven ever wrote. They certainly were the last that he wrote to Schindler. On the back of the note, in another writing (probably Schindler's), the receipt is given in pencil for the bath with hay steeped in it, ordered by Malfatti, which the poor invalid thought had saved his life. The "learned gentlemen" are Dr. Wawruch and the surgeon Seibert, who had made the punctures.]*

475 - To Moscheles.

Vienna, March 18, 1827.

No words can express my feelings on reading your letter of the 1st of March. The noble liberality of the Philharmonic Society, which almost anticipated my request, has touched me to my inmost soul. [1] I beg you, therefore, dear Moscheles, to be my organ in conveying to the Society my heartfelt thanks for their generous sympathy and aid.

[Say[2] to these worthy men, that if God restores me to health, I shall endeavor to prove the reality of my gratitude by my actions. I therefore leave it to the Society to choose what I am to write for them--a symphony (the 10th) lies fully sketched in my desk, and likewise a new overture and some other things. With regard to the concert the Philharmonic had resolved to give in my behalf, I would entreat them not to abandon their intention. In short, I will strive to fulfil every wish of the Society, and never shall I have begun any work with so much zeal as on this occasion. May Heaven only soon grant me the restoration of my health, and then I will show the noble-hearted English how highly I value their sympathy with my sad fate.] I was compelled at once to draw for the whole sum of 1000 gulden, being on the eve of borrowing money.

Your generous conduct can never be forgotten by me, and I hope shortly to convey my thanks to Sir Smart in particular, and to Herr Stumpff. I beg you will deliver the metronomed 9th Symphony to the Society. I enclose the proper markings.

Your friend, with high esteem,
BEETHOVEN.

*[**Note 1:** A hundred pounds had been sent at once.]*

*[**Note 2:** In the original the words placed within brackets are dictated by Beethoven himself, and were indeed the last he ever dictated--but they are crossed out.]*

476 - Codicil. [1]

Vienna, March 23, 1827.

I appoint my nephew Carl my sole heir. The capital of my bequest, however, to devolve on his natural or testamentary heirs.

LUDWIG VAN BEETHOVEN. [2]

*[**Note 1:** See No. 463. Schindler relates:--"This testament contained no restrictions or precautionary measures with regard to his heir-at-law, who, after the legal forms connected with the inheritance were terminated, was entitled to take immediate possession of the whole. The guardian and curator, however, knowing the unexampled levity of the heir, had a valid pretext for raising objections to these testamentary depositions. They therefore suggested to the maestro, to alter his intentions in so far as to place his property in trust; his nephew to draw the revenue, and at his death the capital to pass to his direct heirs. Beethoven, however, considered such restraints as too severe on the nephew whom he still so dearly loved in his heart [since December of the previous year the young man had been a cadet in a royal regiment at Iglau, in Moravia], so he remonstrated against this advice; indeed he reproached Hofrath Breuning as the person who had suggested such harsh measures. A note, still extant, written by Breuning to Beethoven, shows the state of matters, in which he still maintains, though in moderate language, the absolute necessity of the above precautions. This mode of argument seemed to make an impression on the maestro, who at last promised to yield his own wishes. By his desire, Breuning laid the codicil of three lines before him, and Beethoven at once proceeded to copy it, which was no easy matter for him. When it was finished he exclaimed, 'There! now I write no more!' He was not a little surprised to see on the paper the words 'heirs of his body' changed into 'natural heirs.' Breuning represented to him the disputes to which this destination might give rise. Beethoven replied that the one term was as good as the other, and that it should remain just as it was. This was his last contradiction."]*

*[**Note 2:** Next day, at noon, he lost consciousness, and a frightful death-struggle began, which continued till the evening of March 26, 1827, when, during a violent spring storm of thunder and lightning, the sublime maestro paid his last tribute to that humanity for which he had made so many sacrifices in this world, to enter into life everlasting, which, from his life and actions, few could look forward to more hopefully.]*

www.ingramcontent.com/pod-product-compliance
Lightning Source LLC
LaVergne TN
LVHW091000080826
845145LV00003B/1066

* 9 7 8 1 7 8 9 8 7 4 1 4 3 *